D1571166

THE ENDANGERED BLACK FAMILY
Coping with the Unisexualization and Coming Extinction of the Black Race

by
Nathan Hare
and
Julia Hare

A Black Male/Female Relationships Book
Black Think Tank

1st printing, March, 1984
2nd printing, December, 1984
3rd printing, December, 1985
4th printing, July, 1986
5th printing, April, 1993

THE ENDANGERED BLACK FAMILY

ISBN: 0-9613086-0-5
Published by

BLACK THINK TANK
1801 Bush Street, Suite 127
San Francisco, CA 94109

Bookstores may order direct; at a 40% discount, payable in advance.

Number 1 in the Black Male/Female Relationships Book Series.

Typesetting and layout by Tutankhamun Graphics.

Contents

iii

ORDER OR SUBSCRIBE TODAY

To register your order for the next in The Black Male/Female Relationships Book Series, or to subscribe to Black Male/Female Relationships, send a check or money order for $10, postpaid.

Black Male/Female Relationships
1801 Bush Street, Suite 127
San Francisco, CA 94109

◯ Check here if you want a subscription to the journal.

◯ Check here if you wish the next book in the series and wish to know when it is published.

◯ Check here if you wish both.

Part I: <u>The Deception</u>

Introduction:
For a Better Black Family

The most talked about, but least understood, subject among black Americans today is black male-female conflict. At a national symposium on Homicide among Black Males, sponsored by a federal agency in Washington in 1981, the predominantly black male behavioral and social scientists spent all day peppering their deliberations on the crumbling black marital structure and the need for mass employment of black males, with angry verbal jabs at the infamous 1965 Moynihan Report, apparently unaware that Moynihan had been saying exactly the same things fifteen years before: that there is a trauma somehow in black marital relationships and that one solution, in a patriarchal society at least, might be the need to beef up the economic, at least the employment, clout of black males. (For instance, 60 percent of the black wife beaters are unemployed in Minneapolis, where only about 5 percent of the overall workforce is unemployed).

The only difference in what Moynihan said and what his angry black critics were saying was that Moynihan was concerned with the 25 percent female-headed family rates in 1965, while the black scholars were calling attention to the almost 50 percent (48 percent nationwide and growing) female headed black family rate today. The black social scientists and Moynihan in turn are echoed by white feminist scholars who wish to spotlight the special poverty of female headed families, unmindful that the feminist solutions have merely compounded them. The only difference is that the upper middle class white feminists argue that it is they who should have the jobs, or coterminously, the black female headed poor, in preference to the unemployed black males.

It is the purpose of *The Endangered Black Family: Coping with the Unisexualization and Coming Extinction of the Black Race,* not only to analyze the by now well conceded trouble within the black family (so long denied by defensive black intellectuals in the post-Moynihan hysteria) but also to penetrate the iron conspiracy of silence on the quiet-kept government programs and policies unleashed by Nixon Administration eugenicists, both liberal and moderate alike, exploiting the idea of "women's liberation."

These officials and their demographers were alarmed because they had discerned that, being affluent, white people are not reproducing themselves, even as the black poor and nonwhite hordes continue to multiply. Their anxiety not only was, and is, expressly piqued by the belief that the rising population pressure among the nonwhite poor will lead to social unrest. [See an article, "Abortion: a National Security Isssue," in the August, 1983 issue of The Humanist, reprinted from The American Journal of Obstetrics and Gynecology, written by Stephen Mumford, of the International Fertility Research Program. Mumford backs his claims by quoting the following—often in testimony before the House Select Committee on Population, or the Senate Foreign Relations Committee to the effect that Population Control, in order to keep down rebellion in the developing world and domestically, is America's priority, "the most serious threat to United States security," to use Alexander Haig's words, "than thermonuclear war": Charles Cargill, World Population Society (1974); Former Assistant Secretary of State George W. Ball (1976); Former World Bank President Robert M. McNamara (1977); former Director of the Central Intelligence Agency (CIA) William Colby, (1970s and 1978); Ambassador Marshall Green, then coordinator of population affairs, United States Department of State (1978); Retired Army General Maxwell Taylor; Center for Strategic and International Studies; Lester Brown, the Worldwatch Institute; and others. For his work toward population control, Stephen Mumford received a 1982 Distinguished Service Award from the American Humanist Association, as did in 1983 the feminist Fran Hosken, editor of WIN (Women's International Network) News, who almost killed the National Black Monitor, supplement to more than a hundred black weeklies, because the Monitor would not take back soon enough to suit Ms. Hoskens the statement that Africa, in preference to white feminists, could very well determine its own cultural future.]

The white demographers and eugenicists are concerned, moreover, that the white race may be growing extinct. Calculations have led to the prediction that whites will be in the minority in the United States by the year 2050; in California by the year 2000; and worldwide, by the year 2030, whites will constitute only 15 percent of the earth's human population.

Thus, in the autumn of 1969, when Betty Freidan founder of NOW (the National Organization for Women) and the author of The Feminine Mystique, stood in the twilight of the black consciousness movement and declared that "the blacks had the sixties; [white women] will have the 70's" she was not speaking as a fortune teller, though she would tell our fortune. Forces already in motion, of which she was a part but by no means the architect, would mold our family and therefore our psychological, economic, and sociological fates. However, Betty Freidan, a happily married woman who has subsequently altered the essence of her initial strategy, now that the deed is done, in preparation for her Second Stage, was representing the forces that would seduce and capture the ideas and aspirations of black intellectuals for the next fourteen years.

Black intellectuals allowed the white feminists, in search of their "identities" and practicing "assertiveness," not only to take jobs and income (while raising the standards of living and contributing to inflation in augmenting consumption more than basic production and making two-earner families the norm) to take jobs that could have gone to black males, while the black social scientists made studies funded by the liberal-moderate grant-making establishment to argue whether black women were taking the jobs! While the black intellectuals bought the anti-pathology bias and "positive" thinking of the 1970's white liberal, the white liberal woman was thereby left free to take center stage and cry about the pathology, real and imagined (as in the case of rape) in the white family. For instance, a rapist was declared to be a political animal, when in reality, a rapist is a psychopath, if nothing else; and it is racial psychopathy for white women to exploit the rape issue overwhelmingly victimizing the black urban poor woman in an effort to legitimize the white agenda of cultural change. It is pathetic for black intellectuals to let them, let along to help them. If rape were a political act, the most political people of all would be employing this new tool of power and committing most of the rape. In fact, rape is one of the consequences of the politics of a morally decadent white society afflicting predominantly the low income urban black male and female whose interests continue to be failed and bartered away by the behavioral and social "sciences." Although we ouselves should be seriously trying to solve the problems of black-on-black rape, crime and violence, rape most emphatically will not be solved by white feminists. Indeed, it has increased since the feminists got into the act, despite millions of dollars in government grants and private

10

donations and studies—and it shall increase for the foreseeable future while black intellectuals and leaders continue to fail their roles.

(Readers interested in pursuing how black intellectuals were misled into denying black urban family decay in the name of a false racial pride may see the "Introduction" to Talcott Parsons and K. Clark (eds.). *The Negro American,* 1967, for an account of his organization of black intellectual moderation, under the auspices of the American Academy of Arts and Sciences, in the early, middle and late 1960's, and for the motives behind Parsons' conspiracy and his "strategy of pluralization"; also Erik Erikson's blueprint to emphasize only the strengths or "positives" of black family life presented to the conference set up in 1965 by the planning groups that followed the "private meetings" of the thirty-three scholars handpicked by Parsons expressly to tone down black rebellion since it would have, he believed, dire repercussions for the international goodwill of America, particularly in the rich mines of Africa, if blacks continued to "stir things up" by "making themselves a special case." See also William J. Wilson's analysis of Parson's influences in "the New Black Sociology," in Blackwell and Janowitze, eds., Black Sociologists: Historical and Contemporary Perspectives, 1974; also our own "What Black Intellectuals Misunderstand About the Black Family," *Black World,* March, 1976.

Instead of adopting an honest and deeper study of the problems of the black family, black intellectuals took up the polyanna psychology and social science that would characterize the 1970's. Whenever an oppressed people, begin to feel too weak to fight the real oppressor, they tend to turn away from social combat to concentrate upon patching up their battered self-images and advantages: personal development through human potential workshops, tai-chi, hypnosis, meditation, feel-good therapy, and the

11

like. By tying the esteem and self-concept of the group to a mystique of problem-free adaptability, they become self-centered and apathetic in the face of persistent oppression from without. Thus, while black intellectuals with their condominiums and two-car garages, continued to ferret out and assert the "strengths" of the black family, everywhere we went, black people were crying the blues as male-female conflict mounted and things continued to fall apart. Black intellectuals joined white feminists, or collaborated with them in suppressing all studies and writings finding pathology in the black family. And this would be true at least until the 80's. (See Michael Levin's "Feminism and Thought Control" in the June 1982 issue of *Commentary*. Tony Brown, nationally syndicated columnist, and Sam Yette, author of *The Choice*, also are among those who have charged a current blackout by the publishing industry on meaningful black books).

Meanwhile, also in 1969, Richard Nixon had come to office and, unknown to us at the time, and most people to this day (for the public has never been told), called for legislation on population control, which Congress enacted in 1970. In 1971, Sam Yette, now a Howard University professor and then a *Newsweek* correspondent fired allegedly for his book, *The Choice,* referred to Nixon's efforts (pp. 109-115). Although, Yette did not have available the Commission's final set of recommendations, he nevertheless recognized its genocidal nature even in its embryonic form. Indeed, Nixon is quoted as saying in 1969: "A third measure for which I would ask your support" --and this is the only one the government has *really* tried to have reach the poor "is the Commission on Population Growth and the American Future, which I have proposed to Congress, and which has been most cordially received there, as well as by church and civic organizations throughout the nation. America, I believe, has come to see how necessary it is to be

12

responsibly concerned with the subject. In proposing the Commission, I also declared that it would be the goal of this administration to provide "adequate family planning services within the next five years to all those who want them." There are some five million women in low income families who are in that situation. *But I can report that the steps to meet that goal have already been taken with the adminstration, and the program is underway.*" (Emphasis in the text as quoted by Sam Yette).

Yette reported that the conference itself, White House Conference on Food and Nutrition, December 2-4, 1969), "was worse than a farce. Not only did it dash the hopes of the hungry in a way almost unprecedented, it also succeeded in advancing–against strong sentiments of the poor at the conference -- *the administration's own program of imposing birth control on the Blackpoor."*

After Dr. Alan F. Guttmacher, of the Population Council, had given support to the preliminary recommendations of mandatory birth control to any girl over the age of 13 who requested it, with or without parental consent, and mandatory abortion for any such girl found to be pregnant, and mandatory sterilization of any such girl giving birth out of wedlock for a second time, Fannie Lou Hamer, the black civil rights worker from Mississippi, "still ailing," Sam Yette reports, "and lame from police beatings over the years, was resting on a bench in the lobby of the Sheraton-Park Hotel." On hearing the program being planned inside, "she responded with shock and grave disappointment. "What?!" she exclaimed. "What are you talking about?. . . Where are they carrying on that kind of talk?"

"Hearing the location, and without another word, the gallant lady pulled herself up on a cane and headed for the panel's meeting room. Along the way, she spotted certain black men whom she summoned to follow her. She arrived at the room with about half a dozen bold black men who walked to the front of the room and stood like soldiers. Mrs. Hamer followed them to the front and stood in the center of the panel leaders, demanding to be heard.

"Dr. Lowe yielded.

"She then demanded that the birth control proposal, which had just been adopted, be reconsidered. After a ten-minute oration, spelling out the horror of such a law in the hands of public officials she had known, the resolution was obliterated. After a promise from Dr. Lowe and the panelists that no such resolution would be further entertained, Mrs. Hamer and her black male aides marched out as directly as they had come.

"Quite apparently, a major objective of what was originally called "The White House Conference on Hunger" had failed. However, that tentative failure by no means obscured from the poor a clear attitude which the government would seek to implement as law and policy: *The solution to the hunger problem would not be more food to feed the hungry, but fewer hungry persons to be fed.*"

When Sam Yette made those prophetic revelations in *The Choice, The issue of Black Survival in America*, he was prophetic but had no way of knowing that the Commission would nevertheless be established and would not only "liberalize" the troublesome resolutions in their programming, leaving them if anything more deadly, and sell them as "liberation;" they would do so without ever letting the public know of the existence of the Commission. It is possible to read about it only in the journal of *Family Planning Perspectives*, wherein population control experts and eugenicists are talking among themselves, far removed from the eyes and the ears of the average intellectual, let alone the public. One other book, the only one we have come across, that mentions the Commission on Population Growth and the American Future, is *Great Expectations*, by Charles Harris. *Great Expectations* is a book purporting to explain

14

the population factors involved in the baby boom generations's impact on society. It is endorsed with a sendoff by Charles Westoff, who was executive director of the Commission chaired by John D. Rockefeller, III. Three times the book refers to the Commission, but never so much as hints at its nature or intent, let alone that it had orchestrated the very trends and consequences the book was purporting to explain.

Following Sam Yette's warning in 1971, and our own restricted efforts to be heard in opposition to the white manufacturers of the blinders worn by black intellectuals regarding black family strife since 1969, and just after Nixon fell to the Watergate scandal, the Commission on Population Growth and the American Future revealed its resolutions in the population control journal, *Family Planning Perspectives*. However, hardly anybody other than readers of that journal (wherin the Commission's intentions and plans to propagandize, orchestrate and erect their programmatic solutions are discussed among themselves), appear aware of the Commission's existence. The silence is so effective as to cause knowledgeable persons, when told of its influence, to perch their heads in disbelief.

By 1975, having completed a Ph.D dissertation in clinical psychology on "Black Male/Female Relations (before we switched to "relation*ships*" after people thought we were talking about sex), we continued to push the idea of black male/female relationships as a new area of concentration, suggesting it to black professional and scholarly conventions, sometimes volunteering to present a paper, as in 1975 at the meetings of the national Association of Black Psychologists, held in Boston, and the national Caucus of Black Sociologists, held in San Francisco. We also continued to accept invitations to speak at colleges and local gatherings in remote locales throughout the country, and wrote an editorial commentary, "For a Better Black Family," *Ebony*

15

magazine's Speaking Out feature. Here is what the editorial said:

"If we had to name the most tragic failure of black people historically in the United States, we'd have to point to the relations between black males and black females. Our confusion, our negligence, in this area is both curious and shocking, because the relations between male and female are the most intimate and basic of all human entanglements and the most crucial for the subjugation of a people.

When the Swedish social scientist Gunnar Myrdal (with the collaboration of leading black and white liberal scholars) made his study of *An American Dilemma* during World War II, he found that whites placed sexual and social intimacy first as a source of contention around the issue of black equality while blacks put such matters last. Unfortunately, many black leaders and scholars echoed Myrdal in seeing this contrast as either irrelevant or as a cause for glee and nationwide chuckling. But we suspect that it merely shows that white folks know more about the art of racism than black people know about it. Whites, not blacks, are the professionals in the practice of racism against blacks.

Meanwhile, we are left with an agonizing duality of racism and sexism, which combine to confuse us and to control and defeat out collective thrust. Almost anybody will acknowledge these days that we live in a society that is both sexist (or patriarchal) and racist. In such a society, it was historically the black male who, in the white man's mind, posed the crucial threat to his power and status, who conceivably could take his, the white male's place. However, at the same time as they endeavored to emasculate the black male, they also sought to defeminize the black female. Her beauty was denied, her femininity and her virtues denigrated, and she was robbed of the chance to nestle comfortably on a pedestal of protected womanhood

16

or otherwise to enjoy the privileges of a woman as defined by the white slavemaster society and her own, the slave society. She was not to be a woman any more than a black man could be a man.

Yet black crusaders have attacked inequities in every major social institution in American society except the family (let alone black male-female relations as such). In the area of education, we have fought for school integration and raised the alternative of community control and quality-black-oriented education. In politics, we now have the right to vote, and already have elected mayors, congressmen and women, state legislators and the like. In economics, we have the fair employment laws, "black capitalism," and black left-wing efforts to replace capitalism with socialism. In esthetics, we have excellence in music and entertainment, acting on television, and black movies produced and directed by blacks as well as Hollywood proper. And in religion we have established our own churches and our own denominations, even our own sects, and now are searching for a universal black theology. But what have we done for the black family collectively, aside from asserting the notion of its strength and tracing its elusive and ancient African roots? This is good anthropology but it is not black reconstruction.

Too many black scholars and intellectuals have tried for shaky reasons in recent years to pretend that all is well with the black family, despite our recognized economic, educational and political deprivation. Appalling is the only word we know that begins to describe the way we have begun to play down the neglect, the psychological effects and the social destruction of the inability to earn an acceptable living. We pretend that somehow we can't see the deadly significance of unemployment and underemployment of the black male—for whom a program of mass employment and reconstruction other than in prisons and military camps is necessary if the black family is ever going to be restructured as a viable leverage in the quest for social and economic elevation. The black male's endeavor to camouflage or overcompensate for his own awareness that society has frustrated his performance of his role too often takes the form of a flight from the family nest.

According to a United States Census report of late July, almost two out of five black families are now headed by females. Never mind the rhetoric to the effect that that may be ideal, ask most of the black females involved instead of the black and white liberal social scientists who live in two-parent, two-car families. Like most indices of social decay, this figure for black female heads of families is more than three times the rate for whites. Black children are about as likely to suffer the loss of at least one parent (usually the father) as not to; among those black families with incomes under $6,000, the figure is nearly all of them —nine out of ten. We love and lose our parental figures too early and too often as children, and this frustration (and conflict) manifests itself in many subtle and complex ways in later adulthood life.

It is no wonder that black males and females are finding it increasingly hard to get along together, but we are ignoring this unfortunate fact in the name of a false racial pride. The problem, the black male-female schism, is complicated further by the inability of the white-dominated feminist movement to answer crucial questions it has raised for black female liberation. We, for our part, have failed to incorporate black women's liberation as an integral part of the general black movement (as against sporadic black female efforts which, in their simple mimicry of white feminists, are too often hostile and contrary to the black male). The problem in turn is compounded by the displaced power struggle that presents itself between the black male and the black female.

We propose that we begin to establish black love groups (psychological workshops, group therapy) to begin to elevate black love groups to the status of a social movement reminiscent of, but by no means mimicking, the popularity of so-called encounter groups among alienated and disaffected white individuals during the late 1960's. In this way we can begin to iron out our differences and our difficulties and perhaps to arrive ultimately at a workable solution. Understand us, we are not trying to say that black people as a group are sick. But it may be correct to say that a black person in our society doesn't have to be sick in any way to experience problems in life and living requiring professional guidance. It is clear to us that at the same time as black love group participants work out their personal conflicts, they would indirectly contribute to the general solution of black male-female conflicts so vital to the race as a whole in the crucial years ahead.

We believe that through black love groups we may learn to love again (that is, to feel loved), to love ourselves, and therefore one another). We already know how to hate one another."

We had not reckoned on the powers of thought control and the devices and deceit that those who would generate division and diversion in the black race could muster to perpetuate the destruction of the black family.

This book is dedicated to the endeavor to resist that destruction and to build a better black family, for a better love among black people everywhere.

Feminist Hype:
The Emergence of the White Bourgeoisie-Woman as Sexual Pioneer and Liberator

In the prevailing sexual liberation movement, what goes for revolution is often radical but not geared to genuine socio-political transformation and in fact takes the place of basic revolutionary struggle. Moreover, the very solutions which white radicals and their black followers hold out as alternatives to the despicable nuclear family and the corrosion of the lamented extended family of the agrarian past are but unconscious adaptations to the demands of a post-industrial society.

Such correctives will serve to further nuclearize (fragmentize and atomize) the family unit. For instance: anti-male (even anti-maternal) feminism, the rationalization of the rise in single parenthood and the general romanticizing of ephemeral relationships; the advocacy of unisexism and unisexualization, ultra-permissive childrearing and its alienation of parent-child relations and corrosion of family loyalties.

Understand us, many of these diversions represent justifiable individual rights and freedoms. For example, there is nothing wrong with being a black female single-parent—and one rightfully makes the most of any situation in which she/he finds herself. But there is something wrong with why a black woman is so much more likely to experience the single parent situation, why one race can freely imprison, send off to military duty, unemploy, underemploy, and otherwise destroy the oppressed black woman's eligible male supply. Also there is something wrong with glorifying this problem instead of rising up to change it. People will speak here of "options," but forced or unintended options must be called by some other name.

Besides, this conflict, this confusion of individual rights and collective liberation, is at the heart of our present apathy and inactivity. For, whenever an oppressed people begins to feel too weak to fight their social oppression, they will tend among other things to turn away from social combat alternatively to patch up their own battered selves, to personal growth and self-satisfaction in the name of social change.

In our time this comprises a variety of feel-good maneuvers and endless contemplations of our inner lives and the cosmos—meditation, primal therapy, astrology, tai-chi, born-again religious enthusiasm, fanatical dietary messianism and somatized narcissism, plus encounters of every kind in the realm of the parapsychological. In the arena of sexual liberation itself, middle-aged affluent housewives who have smugly occupied the pedestal all their lives will now saunter out and seize a job that could have gone to somebody who needs it in order now to focus in on "finding my own identity."

Which brings us to the second major premise in our thesis that the current sexual liberation movement does not represent a revolutionary alternative to the socio-political status quo but merely an unconscious adaptation to it. We refer in this instance specifically to the middle class white women's liberation movement. What follows has nothing to do with the issue of the obvious justice of women's rights and freedoms. On the contrary, many of the ultra-assimilationist feminist efforts to erase gender indentity and biocultural distinctions between male and female (mistakenly making sameness synonymous with equality) appear ungrounded in any belief that women have the right to exist as full human beings and to enjoy all human prerogatives as women, to be proud of their own bodies and their differences and to realize their full (even when divergent) potentialities and contributions—without having to first become men, or even like men. The question, then is when and why did this movement arise and whether its consequences are revolutionary or reactionary.

Leaving aside for the moment its functions as a diversionary alternative to black rebellion, let us look at how the women's liberation movement arose simply out of and corroborated forces already in motion and sympathetic to the over-industrialized status quo. To begin with, Western industrialization not only separated home and work; it also pushed women out of the home (with its mechanization of domestic chores and even the suckling of babies) but also pulled women into the workplace where they supplied the army of clerical and related work demanded by the mushrooming bureaucratization of society. However, even when the white middle class woman was privatized in the home, and childrearing and homemaking had become fulltime occupations, black and poor women had already long been forced out of the home for the economic survival of their families.

It was the growing amenability of women to the work force, the rising standard of living's demand for dual breadwinning, the declining birthrate following the initial post-World War II baby boom, compensatory preoccupation with birth control and "zero population growth," plus the relentless pruning down and nuclearization of the family unit, that flung women into the work force, where feminisim could feed upon decaying family norms and the vola-

23

tile, shifting sexual mores. Whereas earlier women's movements had tended to focus on a single issue such as suffrage, the most conspicuous difference assumed by the movement of the 1960's and 1970's, aside from more global demands, was its attack on the very idea of "feminine" and even gender identity itself.

But of course the more things changed the more they remained the same. For the white women's movement arose not so much in the service of revolutionary structural change as in assertion of an ideology of self-expression and the search for personal satisfaction and identity. The do-your-own-thingism that arose in the new apathy of the 1970's was the *sine qua non* of the women's liberation ideology, where greater sexual license and variety were seen as synonymous with women's elevation and equalization, when in fact these were the very privileges most men had been lusting for all their lives. Besides, these new sexual liberties could readily be tolerated by the state as a psychological safety-valve to true revolutionary steam in the manner described by Herbert Marcuse in his *Eros and Civilization*. And so, a number of women were able to alter their personal lives but made hardly any structural change that was not already in the cards of mass urbanization and industrialized societal evolution.

Now get this: as a matter of fact, the relative median year-round fulltime earnings for white women actually decreased by comparison to white men between 1963 and now while black women made tremendous gains relative to black men. In other words, the feminist movement enabled the white male to keep his act together, to retain his position of superordinance to his woman, while further decimating the black male's ability to prevail and compete in a perpetually patriarchal society, thus aggravating the alienation and disunity of black male and black female.

Our computations from census data additionally reveal

that the white male did not alter appreciably his participation in the labor force since 1963, nor that of the black female (who has always had to work to make up for the relative psycho-socio-economic suppression of her man). But almost to the exact extent that the white female has entered the labor force the black male has been pushed out of it, with obvious consequences for black sexual and family relationships.

Now the white woman outnumbers the black male roughly a dozen to one and is about twice as likely to have been graduated from college. Thus for every black male college graduate there are about two dozen white female college graduates. This, plus the white female's proximity and intimate relationship to the white male foreordained her privileged access to the necessarily limited new jobs. Consequently, if we take black college graduates in urban places (where most now live) between the ages of 19 and 44, for every 100 males there are 54 extra females. On top of this, the white woman as a whole, though not in the professional class as such, faces an eligible male shortage of her own and accordingly slips over to further deplete the vanishing black male supply. For even when the white female is not a college person, she prefers to marry the college level black male.

Let us make no mistake about this thing of sex and race. In a patriarchal society which is both sexist and racist, it is the male of the oppressed species who, in the ruling male's mind, conceivably would take his place. From the moment of his first encounter with the darker races, the white male has feared exclusion and inadequacy in any unrestrained sexual interaction of the races. Historically, he has used the white female as an object and a force, simultaneously and variously extended and withheld, as a distraction to the aspirations of the black race.

The black male has been the main object of this spi-

25

dery lure, but it has been the black woman who has been left to bear the acute emotional brunt and social trauma of the destruction and diversion of the black male's collective thrust. For an analysis of how the feminst movement itself has been employed by the West in its neo-colonial policies of African domination, we would ask the reader to see Achola O. Pala's "Definitions of Women and Development: An African Perspective," as well as Frantz Fanon's chapter on "The Unveiling of Algier's" in his studies in *A Dying Colonialism.*

While it is true that the white race has a family problem, it is of a wholly different character; and, whereas the white race has a woman problem, the black race has a woman problem and a man problem. Hence, it was altogether ludicrous, even if cute and cunning, when the white feminists of the 1960's and 1970's sought to exploit the spirit, the metaphor and the rhetoric of the black movement but refused to face up to their own racism.

A salient case in point is the current rape scare perpetrated (according to an analysis reported in *Social Problems,* the journal of the Society for the Study of Social Problems) as an opportunistic appeal to press coverage and sympathy for the feminist movement despite the fact that the incidence of rape had not mushroomed. Available figures show about 8 out of 10 rapists and rape victims to be black. Rape is a problem in black male-female relationships, but the black woman is getting raped while the white woman is doing the screaming. More white males in absolute number rape black women than black males rape white women. Indeed, as far back as the 1940's, when the white male's exploitation of the rape-scare smokescreen clearly soared, the Southern white liberal Lillian Smith reported in her famous book, *Strange Fruit,* that a white woman's chances of getting raped by a black man are about as great as her probability of being struck by a bolt of lightning. Yet the

26

APA Monitor, the official organ of the American Psychological Association, reports that a $21.7 million research boost was recommended by the President's commission and requested by the president includes $6 million for rape; which equals the amount allotted for all minority mental health and is greater than the mere $4 million advanced for urban mental health problems.

Yet the rape scare is so tied to the black male in the popular mind (and the white woman knows this) that it will further defame him there and in the image of his woman and his own. It is a part of the neo-racism now emerging, about which there is so much we could say; but we must turn now to black sexual liberation proper.

The idea of black sexual change has mainly amounted to fallout and reactions, including overreactions, to white norms and notions. In 1971 we raised a cry in the pages of The Black Scholar: "Will the Real Black Man Please Stand Up?" There we said in part:

> This is the era of liberation, and because it is the era of liberation, the black man will be able to bring the woman along in our common struggle, so that we will not need a black women's liberation movement. In the struggle to reassert our black manhood, we must sidestep the trap of turning against our women and they, in retaliation, turning against us. The black woman is, can be, the black man's helper, an undying collaborator, standing up with him, beside her man.

This notion of incorporating the idea of black women's liberation into the black movement (but not to take the place of it) was the same view that V.F. Lenin had expressed when the bourgeois feminist movement threatened the Russian socialist initiative. Our national survey of black women reported in *Transaction* (now *Society*) in 1969 had already noted the black woman's wary stance toward the white feminist and a feeling that the black woman's fate was inextricably bound to that of the black male.

However, forces were already in motion which would cripple the aspirations of the black female *and* the black male. The signal was sounded in 1969, though of course it did not begin there, by Betty Friedan. Friedan's *The Feminine Mystique* and her role in founding the National Organization for Women are credited with launching the women's liberation movement (in the way that Dr. Spock is thought to have initiated permissiveness in childrearing). Friedan was quoted as saying: "The blacks had the sixties; women will have the seventies." It was true that whites for years had been thrashing about for ways and means to seize the revolutionary initiative. This effort sprang up during the passive resistance and sit-in movements but escalated with the open rejection of white females and white control by a black power-minded SNCC and the overall turn toward a separatist black consciousness.

The Vietnam issue, "human rights" briefly, ecology, and at last women's liberation, contended for the revolutionary initiative then held by blacks. In women's liberation, at last whites had a hook. Unlike Lenin, who wished to incorporate the bourgeois women's movement into the socialist movement, white male marxists as a group appeared quite willing to embrace this less risky form of "struggle." It permitted white males to keep a bigger slice of the American pie in the family while they engaged in counterinsurgent combat with their poor middle class wives, their mothers, their daughters, their lovers; or, as many preferred, joined them as comrades *sans* arms. The white male may be the common oppressor of the black race and the white woman, but the white woman sleeps with the enemy.

With white women we cannot seriously talk about a genuine revolutionary seizure of power or, for lack of a better phrase, any true territorial imperative. We can merely speak of bio-cultural change, or as we have seen,

28

individual self-expression. Western society has always been prepared to grant individual rights and freedoms as over against collective or social transformations. The black race can exist apart from whites, without them biologically. Poor people conceivably could exist and propagate without the rich. But women are not a biologically autonomous population and could not long exist and perpetuate themselves without men, nor of course visa-versa. It is antinature and therefore anti-human merely to suggest this fantasy. Human cloning may one day be accomplished (presumably "in his image"), but we ourselves are not afraid to say that we believe it is neither necessary nor desirable.

Anyway, the now quietly kept secret of the black race's *man* problem was a thorn in the side of the white women's liberation movement and a reason for the opposition and resistance to an honest appraisal of the systematic destruction of the black family. Thus white scholars fell in behind America's number one sociological theorist Talcott Parsons (who expressly wished to calm the black stir) and psychoanalyst Erik Erikson, after they met under the initial auspices of the American Academy of Arts and Sciences, in a movement to hoodwink black intellectuals into denying black family "pathology" and to searchout and extol elusive strengths.

When once they had engaged the black intelligentsia in this happy-Negro, I'm okay-you're-okay, Norman-Vincent-Peale-power-of-positive-thinking defense mechanism of denying and overlooking black family decay while hunting down and showing off salvaged "strengths," the white feminists, aided and abetted by their male scholars (including of course those who most conspicuously harped on black family strengths) were left free to stress pathology in the white family.

This conspiracy of silence about the destruction and oppression of the black family, this shortsighted and gross intellectual dishonesty, was necessary because a forthright analysis of the black family would inevitably point to the relative suppression of the black male and a contradiction of the simplistic anti-male theme of white feminism and that there were more white women in a position to exploit black men by far than black men so situated to oppress white women. Above all, an honest examination of the black family would reveal perhaps the most painful problem of the black woman—that somebody is depleting, alienating, stealing and otherwise threatening the extinction of her male.

The black woman's greatest cry, if you will only talk to her sometimes and listen, is that she too often lacks a strong black male to stand beside her. She feels impelled too often to serve as the "backbone" of her family and to fullfill the formidable obligation of "both mother and father" to her children. This predicament—and the denial and denigration of her beauty—has resulted from efforts to defeminize her as the white oppressor simultaneously struggled to emasculate (lest we forget) the oppressed black male.

The reason of course is that in order to subjugate you must first dehumanize and this is accomplished best by destructuring the most intimate and basic of all human relations, the relation between male and female. Inasmuch as the slave cannot be a full human being and at the same time a slave, an oppressed female cannot be a full human being (that is, a woman, however her contemporary society may define that) any more then the oppressed male can be a man. What is the source of these new schemes of subjugation and where have they emerged?

Part II: Blueprint and Program for Genocide

Unisexualization:
The Federal Government's
Program of Black Genocide

By now it is clear to the most of us that the history of the European and of Europe's most powerful descendant, white America, has been a history of destruction. Exploiting the machine (including the weapons of war) to dominate the other races and to control the environment, the white man has been nevertheless tripped up by his own advantage. In controlling the environment, he distorts the environment, is anti-nature. But, inasmuch as the human being is also an animal, a part of nature, the culture of the European is anti-human.

While plundering and destroying the earth, he also destructures the human social fabric and its most basic and intimate human relations. Secretary of the Interior James Watt is not a lone, divergent warrior, he is merely his culture's official environmental embodiment today.

Now, the white society is poised to distort the very nature of the human being. We refer here to a process of *unisexualization.* By unisexualization, we do not mean homosexuality, let alone the civil rights of homosexuals, though homosexuality is one conspicuous element or phenomenon being promoted (as we shall see later) in the present scheme of the manufacture and production of unisexuality. In "unisexualization," we refer instead to what is being done to the *hetero*sexuals.

33

The August 30, 1982 issue of Time magazine carries a cover story, "The New Ideal of Beauty," proudly congratulating the American woman for a decade of progress in approaching, through barbells, the musculature of the male. Unisexual fashions, coiffures and toiletries (even sex-change surgery) are now normalized; and this is only the beginning. The processs is aggravated in our time by a felt need on the part of the status quo to keep down population growth in order to dampen racial pressure, and, simulataneously, to avoid the redistribution of the earth's resources.

Although it is true that the nature of European and Euro-American (Western) society had, in the course of industrialization, nuclearized and disintegrated the family structure, these changes appeared capable of being incorporated into the social fabric without any more disruption of basic social values than the great migrations from rural farms to urban factories had wrought. Most significant among these family changes was the growing tendency of married women to work outside the home, born of the mechanization of household appliances and the need for a large supply of cheap and efficient labor in the metropolitan marketplace. However, this trend was cunningly exploited by the architects of unisexualization. These included population eugenicists ("the new scientific racist"), Zionist elements and, finally and most compellingly, the achievement of fullscale adoption of the program by the federal government under the Nixon administration. The Common thread uniting the often diverse interests was the desire to keep down the population growth of the poor and, particularly, the black and Third World populations here and elsewhere, on grounds that easing population pressure would eliminate the pressure-cooker antecedents of war and rebellion which came to characterize the 1960s but were portended as early as World War I.

In the minds of imperialists, population control (which

eventually discovered the effectiveness in that end of a program of unisexualization) was the alternative to war and open genocide, in the interest of avoiding the alternative of a redistribution of wealth and fundamental changes in the socioeconomic order. Instead, they employed the technology (already disrupting the environment of the earth) to alter the very conceptualization of the human being.

Upon the technology of nuclear war was added the technology of the total nuclearization and distortion of the family, through weight-lifting or body-building programs for women and surgical sex-change operations, as well as the denial and systematic elimination of gender differences and aspirations. The technology of surgery (tubal ligation, abortion, etc.) has emerged as the major approach to birth control, combining with biomedical research, test tube babies, and the pill (though not without unanticipated side effects). All of this is undergirded by a deliberate program of propaganda and thought control around the white feminist hook.

Understand that there is a difference between *birth control* per se, which can make the life better for some individuals and their families, and the exploitation of the idea of birth control for genocidal and racist limitation and decimation of an entire group by another—i.e. *population control.* (For detailed accounts of the way in which the population control unfolded, with racist implications all along the way, see Allan Chase, *The Legacy of Malthus: The Social Costs of the New Scientific Racism.* New York: Alfred A. Knopf, 1977, and Elasah Drogin, *Margaret Sanger: Father of Modern Society,* Coarsegold, CA: CUL Publications, 1980). In this treatment we must necessarily be brief, in order to move more quickly to more recent and sinister developments.

And yet, despite the fact that the population eugenicists have known that improved educational and economic conditions lead to a downspin in the birth rate, they chose instead to adopt the approach, not of elevating the blacks and the poor, but of eliminating and "controlling" their numbers (as we shall see later).

However, since the adoption of a worldwide program of unisexualized population control by the United States government and the World Bank and their allies, the economy has appeared to suffer exceedingly more, in unisexualization and a retrenchment of the class inequities. (It is also probably that the feminist aspect of the unisex-utilization program allowed whites to seige back the revolutionary initiative from the 1960s—more about this later— and continues to divide, or further divide, black male and female as well as to provide social legitimacy for the long decimation, historically, of the black male). Note that, in the same way that there is a difference between birth control and population control, there also is a difference between better working conditions, and societal rewards for the emerging female labor force (or "equal rights" for women as women, without having first to become more and more like men nor to eliminate maleness and femaleness) and the current anti-gender white feminist movement tendency to seek the unisexualization of others.

Let us go back, then, to the beginning of the emergence in our time of both feminism and population control, as background and introduction to the specific program of unisexualization adopted under the administration of Richard Nixon and, by now, not only effectively assimilated by the liberal-moderate white establishment but also, increasingly, by the black intelligentsia. This is due, aside from opportunism, to a vast, and grave ignorance of the meaning and the motivation of architects of unisexualization in the Western World.

Irving Howe tells how feminism as a movement or ideology had touched a number of young Jewish women, as Zionism grew stronger after World War One, but that feminism captured mainly those young women moved to rebellion by socialism, though, like Margaret Sanger, they tended to turn to oppose the very right of the poor to exist, let alone to thrive. Like many Jewish teenagers, Golda Meir, growing up in Milwaukee, ran away in order to assert her independence. She eventually was to become Prime Minister of Israel. Bella Abzug, according to *Current Biography*, was a Zionist leader while a student at Hunter College.

Just last summer, in the June issue of *Ms* magazine, edited by Gloria Steinem, there are two articles openly defending Zionism. One is written by a Ms editor, Letty Cotlin Pogrebin. It is called, predictably, "Anti-Semitism in the Women's Movement" since its inception, as is well known, a Jewish-led and dominated movement, kicked-off in our time by Betty Freidan's publication of *The Feminine Msytique* and founder of The National Organization for Women (NOW), though, recently, now that the deed is done, she has entered a "second stage" of returning to an appreciation of the family as the feminists shaped by the Nixon commission view her with scorn and continue the goal of unisexualization. The other article is called similarly "Anti-Semitism at the Copenhagen's Women's Conference" and its author is anonymous.

The *Ms* editor confesses, unsolicited by any reader, that she feels her Jewishness more deeply than her womanness (she feels her Jewishness more deeply than her womanness) but nevertheless condemns black women for similarly putting their blackness first, not to mention their Africanity. Thus, some of the black women the editor of *Ms* desparages for "anti-Semitism" are: Poets Iva E. Carruthers, Carole Clemmons Gregory, and Judy Simmons; Esther E. Edwards, Director of the Regional Office of the National Human Rights Caucus; Sherry Brown, president of the Frederick Douglas Community Improvement Council of Anacostia

37

(in Washington, D.C.); and Thelma Thomas Daley, past president of the Delta Sigma Theta sorority!

On the cover of that issue of *Ms* is a picture of black novelist Alice Walker, now a contributing editor of *Ms* (which has hungered for a token black feminist catalyst since Michelle Wallace , appearing on the cover as a previously unknown 27-year-old unsung and essentially unpublished writer to announce the publication of *The Black Macho*, became a household name, but nevertheless bombed when black people surprisingly but encouragingly rejected this sinister effort to replace the old "black matriarch" villian with the "black macho," when they both suffer a common enemy with whom the white woman sleeps).

Also in 1912 appeared the book, *The Woman Movement*, by a Swedish feminist, Ellen Key, who was to influence Margaret Sanger, "the father of modern society." Sanger also came under the influence of Havelock Ellis, the sexologist, who published the year before his book, *The Problem of Race Regeneration* and introduced Sanger to the eugenic movement. Ellis had written that "paupers not be given Poor Law relief unless they submitted to 'voluntary' surgical sterilization." According to Drogan, Sanger and Ellis fell into an affair when Havelock's wife, Edith, was away on a lecture tour to help with her husband's debts. After Havelock wrote Edith about Margaret and, upon returning to England, believing she had lost her husband to Maragret Sanger, Edith attempted suicide. David M. Kennedy (Birth Control in America) suggests that Havelock's ideas on sex and marriage also led to Margaret's divorcing William Sanger. In 1922, she married J. Noah Slee, owner of 3-in-One Oil, who "became the principle source of funds for the birth control movement. Soon Sanger, who coined the term "birth control" and founded the first birth control clinic as well as Planned Parenthood, was embracing racist notions such as the suggestion in a Depression era issue of the *Birth Control Review* which she edited as a "clearly laid out plan for peaceful genocide" *calling it* "Plan for Peace." Her proposals included a stern and rigid policy of sterilization and segregation to persons "known to be detrimental to the stamina of the race." In years to come Sanger would consort with known racists such as Lothrop Stoddard, a father of the modern scientific racism and well-known author of *The Rising Tide of Color Against White World-Supremacy.* Others would follow (some of whom we shall meet later). However, see books by Allan Chase and Elasah Drogin, already cited, for compelling accounts and documented details of the racist and other sinister "genocidal" motives of Magaret Sanger and population eugenicists of the population control movement that would emerge and flourish to this day.

1955. The birth rate in the U.S. entered a consistent decline which, by 1971, would be reported by the U.S. Bureau of the Census to be the lowest U.S. live birth rate ever recorded.

1958. The U.S. shift in policy regarding fertility control begins in New York City, where a campaign emerged to permit contraceptive prescription in the city's municipal hospitals where the poor and many blacks were treated.

1959. A presidential committee recommends that the United States "provide assistance on population programs to other nations requesting it."

1961. The John F. Kennedy administration begins to express the government's increased concern for population *control.*

President Kennedy appoints a Presidential Commission on Women, with Eleanor Roosevelt, social feminist but not a unisexist, as chair. However, Mrs. Roosevelt soons dies, whereupon she is replaced by Esther Peterson, Director of the Women's Bureau.

Hugh Moore, of the Hugh Moore Fund, brought about the merger of Margaret Sanger's Planned Parenthood Federation with his own World Population Council.

This was also the year of Margaret Sanger's last public appearance. However, Hugh Moore, her associate and also president of the Dixie Cup Company, after literally carrying her off the stage at the Waldorf Astoria dinner held by the Planned Parenthood World Population, will carry on very well for her in the ensuing decade.

1963. Talcott Parsons, the number one sociological theorist, widely regarded as a conservative in sociological circles, issues a summons, under the auspices of the American Academy of Arts and Sciences, saying that the "Negro" is threatening America's international good will (with implications for gold mines, diamonds, etc. and other resources in Africa) by "making themselves a special case" and "stirring things up too much." Parsons issues directives to the thirty-three scholars, some with interlocking roles on a number of crucial population and eugenic groups we will encounter later, ordering them to drop everything for "private meetings" on what the Academy was said to regard as the most important issue since the arms control symposium five years earlier.

Betty Freidan publishes *The Feminine Mystique.*

Congress adopts an Amendment to the Foreign Assistance Act authorizing use of funds for "research into problems of population growth."

1964. Daedalus (the official organ of the American Academy of Arts and Sciences) publishes a special issue on women which includes sociologist Alice Rossi's pioneering feminist work.

The Civil Rights Act officially ends segregation in public accommodations; includes sex as well as race and creed in its language.

The Equal Pay Act for women is passed.

1965. Daedalus publishes reports of the Parsons conference, including the embryo of the Moynihan Report, as well as Erik Erikson's blueprint for denying pathology and emphasizing strengths.

Led by Whitney Young, president of the Urban League, black intellectual integrationists recoil against the Moynihan Report (including its call for the mass employment of black males) on grounds that Moynihan had assaulted their image. White social scientists begin to publish emphasis on the positives, the strengths, of black families, as Parsons had wished.

The U.S. Supreme Court and five states begin to endorse the dissemination and use of contraceptive materials.

The Federal Administration begins to join the movement "under pressure from Congress and President Johnson, now growing concerned with the Vietman crisis.

The first federal agency to put the new policy into operation was here in the United States in the form of the Office of Economic Opportunity (OEO).

As part of its War on Poverty program, OEO begins to make grants to community agencies to finance "voluntary" family planning projects. Some city health departments begin to provide family planning services on a limited basis.

1966. In Washington, D.C., Betty Freidan forms the National Organization for Women (NOW). Among its most notable proposals are the ERA and "the right of women to control their reproductive lives."

By now, Hugh Moore has rebuilt the once faltering Population Reference Bureau and is raising a one-half million dollar annual budget.

1967. All states now have Commissions on the Status of Women.

Congress begins to prod the "reluctant" administrative agencies and amends the Economic Oppportunity Act to designate family planning for special emphasis in the War on Poverty program.

Houghton-Mifflin and Beacon Press both issue reprints of the *Daedalus* special issues on Parsons, with an introduction by Parsons setting forth his conspiracy of 1963-65 and his strategy of mobilization.

The Social Security Act is amended to allocate "at least six percent of funds appropriated for maternal and child health programs to family planning service projects." Congress meanwhile amends the Foreign Assistance Act "to designate funds for aid on family planning and population programs to other nations requesting it."

From this year forward, the federal government has "sought to increase the availability of family planning to low-income couples, largely through project grant programs carried out by the HEW's National Center for Family Planning Services and by the Office of Economic Opportunity."

1968. By now, over one-third of all Puerto Rican women of childbearing age are sterilized, through an industrialization program started there in the 1930's, "Operation Bootstrap," with its heavy emphasis on sterilization. Hispanic women in New York City are more than six times as likely to be sterilized as whites, according to the Committee for Abortion Rights and Against Sterilization Abuse. The Committe spokesperson also told some years later how Dr. R. Ravenholt, while head of the United States Office for Population in the State Department, observed that the most challenging epidemic in the 20th century was the epidemic of people.

Howard Moore takes out full-page ads in *The New York Times, The Wall Street Journal, Time, Fortune,* and *The Washington Post,* calling the Pope, the Bishops, and the Catholic Church itself "a major menace to civilization as we know it." They declare that "the population bomb is the single most important problem facing the world today." Among the signatories are William Shockley, James Cagney, Kingsley Davis, Robert McNamara, an official of the Chase Manhattan Bank, Elmer Roper of Roper polls, and a host of liberal and conservative eugenicists.

Prentice Hall publishes, *Black Families in America*, by Andrew Billingsley. In the introduction, Billingsley openly acknowledges his indebtedness to Parsons and "mainstream sociology." It will become the Bible for black intellectual study of the family in the 1970's. Other white forefathers of the I'm-okay-you're-okay "strengths-of-black families" focus were: Elizabeth Herzog (1966); Robert Coes (1964), also a member of the Parsons-Erickson group; Jesse Bernard (1966); Frank Reissman (1966); and Elliott Liebow (1967). After Billingsley had laid down his pen for administrative work at Howard University and, in turn a Southern black college presidency, white scholars took the lead again, emerging as the messiahs to back up the black intellectuals' endeavors to ferret out the positives while denying the negative aspects of racial oppression and black institutional decimation done by a racist white society. The opportunism of that, aside from feelings of inferiority, is that, if you don't see anything wrong, you don't have to do anything to make things right, to cry out against an oppression that leaves no mark. The name of the white fellow who wrote the book on *"Victimology"* escapes us now, but the white messiahs, revered to this day by black intellectuals (and on whose work they rest their case most frequently) are Gutman, Scarzoni, Stack and even the liberal-conservative but self-styled marxist, Eugene Genovese.

The Women's Equity League, a group of white academic and professional women, is established, also the Women's Political Caucus, led by Bella Abzug, Goria Steinem, and Betty Freidan. Others such as The Feminists say they regard *hetrosexual* intercourse as oppressive and permit only a third of their members to be married or to live with men.

1969. Richard Nixon is inaugurated in January. It is winter in Washington.

Nixon issues a Message to Congress on Population Growth, requesting appropriate legislation.

Betty Freidan warns that "the blacks had the 60's; women will have the 70's."

COINTELPRO (The Counter Intelligence Program) of the FBI to disrupt and divide black militant leaders and organizations, is in full swing, and, unknown also at the time, the Watergate Era.

PRIVATE MEMO

On March 11, 1969, a memorandum is sent to Bernard Berelson, President of the Population Council, sent by Frederick S. Jaffe, then Vice President of Planned Parenthood World Federation. The memo is later found in Federick S. Jaffe's papers on "Activities Relevant to the Study of Population Policy for the U.S." It is in the form of a descriptive table called "Examples of Proposed Measures to Reduce U.S. Fertility, by Universality or Selectivity of Impact." That is, some techniques would be visited upon all groups, indiscriminantly, while others would be narrowly enforced on selected groups. These techniques, in addition to measures already present in 1969, such as family planning, would include payments to encourage contraception, sterilization and abortion. Others would be more explicit and sinister, manifesting a goal of manufacturing and producing the unisexualized society already emerging in our time.

Among these measures seen as having "universal" impact, were so-called "Social Constraints." These included: 1) "Restructure family," a) "postpone or avoid marriage," b) "alter image of ideal family size," 2) "compulsory sex education for children," encourage increased homosexuality," 3) "educate family limitation," 4) "fertility control agents in water supply," and 5) "encourage women to work."

Under "Selective Impact Depending on *Socio-Economic Status [this is us]*, we find these measures: 1) Modify tax policies: a) substantial marriage tax, b) "child tax," c) "tax marriage more than single," d) "remove parents tax exemption," e) additional taxes on parents with more than one or two children in school f) "reduce/eliminate paid maternity benefits," "reduce/eliminate children's or family allowances," "Bonuses for delayed marriage and greater childspacing," "eliminate welfare payments after two children."

For families in "Chronic Depression" (socio-economic): 1) "Require women to work and provide few child care facilities," 2) "limit/eliminate public-financed medical care, scholarships, housing, loans and subsidies to families with more than 2 children."

Finally, under the "Social Controls," there are: a) "compulsory abortion of out-of-wedlock pregnancies," b) "compulsory sterilization of all who have two children except for a few who would be allowed three," c) confine childbearing to only a limited number of adults, d) "stock certificate type permits for children."

Under "Housing Policies": a) "discouragement of private home ownership," b) "stop awarding public housing based on family size."

You will have noticed that some of these measures will have genocidal potential for black people in that they affect the lower socioeconomic groups in gross and subtle degree. By now, some of the policies above are already being proposed by the Reagan administration. However, the Berelson-Jaffe memorandum is only the kernel.

Let us continue our chronological revelations.

Kay Millette publishes *Sexual Politics*.

45

1970. Kay Millett and NOW leaders hold a press conference openly merging the feminist and the lesbian ideals. Firestone's *Dialectics of Sex* (and bi-sex and uni-sex) is issued.

Congress passes the Family Planning Services and Population Research Act, picking up the recommendations of the previous adminstration and authorizing $382 million for a three-year program of services and research.

Congress enacts legislation (responding to a 1969 message, the year before from President Nixon, establishing the historic Commission on Population Growth and the American Future, to be chaired by John D. Rockefeller III and consisting of 24 handpicked members, including Bernard Berelson, of the previous year's Berelson-Jaffe Memorandum. The Commission is charged to come up with a program of population control and population eugenics. In short time, it will.

1971. The black consciousness movement has allowed the white feminists to seize the revolutionary initiative. Militant black intellectuals, following Communist Party leader Angela Davis and the once-ultra-black-nationalist Amira Baraka (LeRoi Jones), switch in droves to marxism. They believe they can organize white workers. Other revolutionaries look away from American oppression to concentrate upon their identities with African struggles on the continent of Africa. Less militant activists turn to electoral politics or to the "human potential" movement, to stress the "positives" and "strengths" of Parsons-Erikson fame, to "get in touch with ME" through personal growth (by which they mean personal acquisition and improvement of social status as well as the pursuit of happiness through jogging, meditation, "looking out for number one," "I'm okay-you're-okay" powers of suggestion and positive thinking, tai-chi, etc. They begin to turn away from combat with their social oppression and to verbalize self-righteous putdowns of "The Sixties," sometimes to laugh in knowing glee. Soon there will be cocaine and the disco and California curls, more and more white women, and for a while at least more Richard Nixon.

THE OFFICIAL BLUEPRINT

The report is out from The Commission on Population Growth and the American Future established in 1970 by the Nixon administration. It is born of a "conscious government policy to help 'improve the quality of life' " through population control, the old idea of the racist eugenicists decades past.

The Commission was chaired by John D. Rockefeller, III, as you may recall. Among its 24 members are: Bernard Berelson (of the Berelson-Jaffe memo of 1969), president of the Population Council; Senator Alan Cranston; Congressman James H. Scheuer; The Executive Vice President of the Ford Foundation; the Vice President of the Amalgamated Clothing Workers of America; and last, but not least, one Charles F. Westoff, the Commission's Executive Director. Remember his name, for we shall encounter him again.

At least one black individual is included: Anita Young Boswell, sister of Whitney Young and a University of Chicago social service professor. Some years later she would show up at a Black Think Tank on the black family organized at Notre Dame in 1978. There she would seek to discount any sexual differences in amenability to the nurturing of infants. She is backed by the other participants at the Conference, who appear wholly unaware or unfamiliar with the contrary writings of pioneer feminst sociologist Alice Rossi in *Daedalus* the previous spring.

Later Ms. Boswell would help to organize the Fifth National Conference of Black Women in Business, held in Chicago, ostensibly put on by the League of Black Women whose President, Barbara Proctor, would later advocate pouring her membership into the almost lily white NOW, after Aileen Hernandez, its only nonwhite head so far, had called NOW "racist." Anyway, the Business conference was backed by whites (one of the white persons on the panel responding to the keynote speaker said later that *her* conference had been "ruined."

The theme of the conference was bringing black women into the bigtime corporations under an anti-male venom, hearing no difference in white and black males, the white panelists, particularly the white male member, were enraged. The conference's representative to Jet magazine than asked for a copy of the speech, as written, typed, took pictures of the speaker and two of the black women leaders and selected a picture for Jet under which the caption had the speaker saying just the opposite of what was said. This appeared in the same issue with a picture of the participants on a National Urban League convention panel, moderated by Tony Brown, dealing with the impact of television and the Mass Media on Black Children, held a week or so later in Los Angeles. This panel included actress Pamela Grier, Producer Norman Lear, Ester Rolle, Raymond St. Jacques, and the same speaker who had been keynote speaker at the Business Women's conference. However, the speaker's complete figure, excepting an arm, had been clipped from the picture as it appeared in Jet, and the account of the participants included no reference to the fact that the speaker in question had even been a member of the panel.

At the Black Business Women's conference, consisting of four or five hundred black women corporate managers and the like, leaders moving on up, they dropped everything at three p.m. sharp and held a disco dance—with only three men present, and one of them gay, who soon fled for his very life.

But let us return to 1972 and the report of the Commission on Population Growth and the American Future, for it was a blueprint that is truly shaping America and the world, in its most essential respects today, impelling us on a stringent course, perhaps soon irreversible, toward a unisexual society in which everybody's freedom will be placed before our own, often with our active collaboration, though not as "voluntarily" as many believe who really have little awareness, but think they have much, about the way in which values are shaped in the computerized, post industrial society.

The Commission was charged expressly with making recommendations "consistent with" the fundamental values of American life" (as the Commission itself described it). In two years, they had determined that: 1) continued population growth would aggravate some of our most pressing social and economic problems; 2) an average two-child family may be achieved "by varying combinations of non-marriage or childlessness." This "non-marriage and childlessness would be "free choice." Abortion and birth control were the means to prevent or terminate unwanted pregnancies on grounds that "a nation's growth should not depend on the ignorance or misfortune of its citizenry" (that is, social disadvantages accruing from class or/and race). Another means advocated by the Commission was increased employment and career-centeredness of women (echoes of the Berelson-Jaffe memorandum, as we shall see frequently); 3) also increasing public conviction and concern (to be orchestrated, of course) over the allegedly negative effects of population growth, at best a popular value judgement but not at all a proven scientific fact); 4) discouraging youthful marriages while encouraging youthful preferences for smaller families, and increased access to abortion and contraception, especially among the black and the poor. In addition, mass media are to be encouraged to downplay traditional sex roles (unisex-ualization) and the eradication of pro-natalist laws and social institutions.

The Commission had further determined that "mainly because of differences in education and income—and a general exclusion from the socio-economic mainstream—unwanted fertility weighs most heavily upon certain minority groups." But, while aware of the socioeconomic factors affecting fertility, the Commission does not propose to correct these inequities but instead rests its case on the notion that "if blacks could have the number of children they want and no more, then fertility and that of the majority white population would be similar." That is, the fertility, though affected by socioeconomic inequities, would be altered by juggling other factors. In this effort the Commission proposes not only the allotment of billions of dollars (at least 1½ billion annually!) but also the transformation and denigration of motherhood, child-bearing, social values, and the very nature of male and female, including the very nature of the female's physical body, now to be embellished with the muscles attainable from barbells, transsexual surgery for willing males. All of this is pegged on the rhetoric of "the freedom of women [though most of the architects of the scheme are men] to control their/her own body [presumably by becoming infinitely more available to service men sexually, then in turn, to be subject to the machinery of surgical birth control and, at the least, the instrumentality of abortion].

Beyond this, the Commission "set as one of its chief goals that the government should help guide internal migration and foreign immigration so as to ease the problems brought about by population movement from farms, towns and villages [black migrants from the South would figure heavily here], and from countries abroad, to our large metropolitan areas."

50

Further, the Commission proposed to *"modify sex and family roles in place of and supplementary to motherhood."* [as the 1969 Berelson-Jaffe memo proposed and as Ms. (in fact Mrs.) Anita Young Boswell would later suggest at the Notre Dame Think Tank on the black family. However, you must understand, reader, that the person being quoted here is the Frederick Jaffe, one-half of the Berelson-Jaffe team—Berelson was on the Commission! Jaffe died the year of the 1978 think tank]. Also, the Commission charges: find ways to "reduce fertility by offering women who want to work the opportunity [sic] to enter the labor force much sooner than they would be able [or inclined] to otherwise." Moreover, "subsidize families who wish to and are *qualified* to adopt children, but are unable to assume the full financial cost of a child's care." (Understand that they are proposing this when they could have proposed to subsidize women who give birth to the children, without stigma, so that motherhood could once again become similar in honor to surrogate mothering—the same for fathering. But this would increase the number of children among the black and the poor, precisely the problem these liberal practitioners of genocide are endeavoring here to solve.

Still other recommendations of the Commission, as reported by Frederick S. Jaffe:

—"assume the highest priority to research in reproductive biology."

—" . . . create a stronger base from which to carry on expanded biomedical, social and behavioral research."

—"provide at least $100 million annually—mostly in federal and partially in private funds—for developmental work on methods of fertility control."

—"halt illegal immigration, which exacerbates many of our economic problems, through an effective enforcement backed up by tougher federal legislation" [as you read recently in the newspaper, the Reagan administration is working on this one right now].

—"develop national population distribution guidelines, including goals, objectives and criteria" [a Carter commission recommended encouraging cross-regional migration and to let the central cities die].

—"develop clean sources of energy production such as nuclear fusion."

The Commission further recommended the enactment of a Population Education Act to help persuade young students to accept the ideas and values of genocidal population control.

—promoting "a diversity of styles of family life in America today ["lifestyles"], including expressly the acceptance "without stigma" the idea of childlessness.

—urge the media "to assume more responsibility in presenting information and education for family living to the public."

—increasing support of research to indentify genetically related disorders [such as sickle cell traits], better screening techniques, etc., and the "exploration of the ethical and moral implications of genetic technology" and genetic screening" [the old line eugenics].

—*women are to be encouraged "to spend less of their lives in maternal functions," instead to "work, seek higher education"* and *"choose roles supplementary to or in place of motherhood."* This alteration "should not be sought on demographic grounds alone, but as a means of offering 'a greater range of *choice!"*

Further:

—it would be "particularly helpful if *marriage, childbearing, and childrearing* could come to be viewed as more deliberate and serious commitments rather than as traditional, compulsory behavior." Thus "attractive work may effectively compete with childrearing and have the effect

52

of lowering fertility."

—that there be a freeze on legal immigration and a crackdown, including "civil and criminal sanctions on *employers* of illegal aliens" or "unauthorized employment." [this is in the hopper right now.] Finally, after urging the ERA be ratified by all states [you can't win them all, at least not the first time around], the Commission called, frankly, for *"long-run national policy of eliminating the ghetto"* while adopting a short-run policy of making the ghetto more pallatable to its inhabitants.

1973. The Nixon administration determines that "hiring preference for blacks to make up for past injustices and oversight is to be replaced by a merit system: civil rights laws are to be enforced less stringently and discrimination clearly in violation of the law must be established for the government to act. The government will no longer attempt to force integration in schools or suburban housing. Busing is to be opposed, if necessary, by a Constitutional Amendment.

The U.S. Supreme Court legalizes abortions.

The American Psychiatric Association declares homosexuality to be normal.

1974. The Census Bureau reports that the decline in fertility in the United States is most pronounced among blacks, American Indians and Mexican Ameircans. [They're getting there]. There is also more family decay, more broken marriages, and more single mothers. Among black females and males in their 20's, the suicide rate will skyrocket.

Richard Nixon bows to the Watergate scandal and resigns to avoid prosecution. Jerry Ford steps in to pardon Nixon, and to carry on. With him is Betty.

1975. U.S. State Department allocates $154 million more dollars for population control.

53

Federal expenses for domestic programs have trippled since the enactment of the Family Planning Services and Population Research Act five years earlier.

Britain passes an Equal Pay Act for women, following by eleven years the action of its most precocious offspring, the United States.

1976. Nonwhite women are three times as likely, by now, as white women to be aborted in the United States.

Late in the spring, about five hundred black women hold a conference at the Berkeley YWCA House. The hidden agenda expressed by conference leaders and voiced openly at the climax of the meeting is to find a way for black women to begin to find alternatives to black men. The answers proposed are: white men and homosexual reinforcements. The only male speaker at the conference expresses opposition, is almost lynched; but the spirit of the conference (and its naive initiative) is split and broken.

Jaffe (of the Jaffe-Berelson team) dies; but his struggle continues.

1977. Carter Administration funds the ERA conference in Houston. Many black women who, until now, had remained suspicious of white women and uneasy with an agenda that is not of their own making nor fitted to their needs instead of the needs of its uppermiddle class white women leaders, will begin to join the feminist movement in leaps and bounds. This is especially true, understandably, of black lesbians but also of intergrationists of every persuasion.

1978. The first test-tube baby, Lucille Brown, is born in London. Others will follow all over the West. It is a part of the bio-medical research advocated by the Commission on Population Growth and the American Future, though previous government bodies had already initiated such research.

The Carter Administration grants an unprecedented

three-year extension to the deadline for passing the ERA (amendment to the Constitution).

1979. Michelle Wallace's divisive diatribe on *The Black Macho and the Myth of the Superblack Woman* is published. She is placed on the cover of Ms. magazine and becomes a household name; but she will not be popular with most black thinkers. On top of anything else that can be said against her, she is violating the black intellectual mythomania derived from the Parsons-Erikson directives, via Andy Billingsley (though innocently enough). Image making is perhaps a better word, more inclusive, than mythomania; for she might have gotten over had she called it " . . . The Myth of the Black Matriarchy," or kept Superblack Woman but left out "Myth."

The Surgeon General, Julius B. Richmond, determines that government physicians will no longer consider homosexuality abnormal.

Reader, do you remember Charles F. Westoff, the Executive Director of the Nixon Administration's Commission on Population Growth and the American Future? The one that determined that in order to keep down fertility and, therefore, to liquidate social unrest among the black and the poor of America and the world, women should be encouraged to work and in general to disdain motherhood; that marriage should be *dis*couraged but childlessness *en*couraged through the education of youth and mass media persuasion, etc. etc.? Well, here he is again in a January 1979 issue of *Psychology Today*. When Richard Esterlin, a demographer at the University of Pennsylvania, concluded that the rapid rise in the labor force participation rate of young women since the 1960s was not due to increasing job opportunities for women (the labor market for younger women had in fact been stronger *before* 1960, according to Esterlin); that the pill as an explanation for birth control was an effect of attitudinal and bio-medical research emphasis and changes more than a cause of women rushing to the labor force; that the women's movement also was a result more then a cause of increased labor force participation of women, Charles F. Westoff, who you may recall was the Executive Director of the Commission on Population Growth and the American Future, was asked what *he* thought of this. Without batting one eyelid, the Watergate era social engineer replied: "It seems to me it misses the whole point . . . There is a hell of an increase in childlessness, I suspect, though it's hard to nail it down . . . A very large proportion of women are working, marriage has gone out of style, and fertility has dropped out of sight. This raises interesting questions about the future of the whole marriage institution." As if Westoff had nothing to do with it; it just happened that way; a matter of your *"choice,"* you see. At least you get a chance to vote between the two candidates they allow you for President; you didn't even get a vote on the program of unisexualization, before the "masters of deceit" had started the wheels of popular belief to turning.

1980. 1,000 black men met "as black men" in the Oakland Arena to organize for the purpose of motivating and resurrecting the black male, toward protecting and providing for his family better, "take care of business," save the black man, woman, and child." For that, they are criticized and denigrated as "sexists" by black feminists and integrationist black male community leaders.

The World Health Organization reports that baby milk formulas outlawed in the United States are being distributed elsewhere, killing an estimated 1 million Third World babies a year.

This is the International Year of Women. The U.S.'s International Conference is held in Copenhagan. U.S. Ambassador to the United Nations, Donald McHenry, attends as the co-head of the predominatly white feminist delegation from the U.S. Bella Abzug, who chaired the 1977 ERA conference in Houston and, with George Bush, kicked off the campaign in 1972 to get the ERA ratified, was there. She made an offer to the 'Iranians they had to refuse. All but four of the 91 nations present vote a resolution to equate zionism with racism. Only Israel, the United States, Canada, and Australia did not agree.

Lynda (Baines) Johnson Robb was there. Soon Betty Ford and Lady Bird herself become ERA leaders.

Rabbi Sol Roth, new president of the Orthodox Rabbinical Council of America, recommends that Jews "eliminate from Jewish Communal life all persons who marry outside the faith" (which includes you) and, further, that the rabbis who perform the ceremony also be purged. Rabbi Alexander M. Schindler, president of the Union of Hebrew Congregations, is much opposed to Rabbi Roth's plan but agrees that intermarriage is a threat to Jewish survival.

Carter bows to Iran and the Middle East crisis. George Bush, of ERA and wide international oil experience for the United States, rides in with Ronald Reagan. This cowboy is for real. Eventually they will be joined by the head of Bechtel.

1981. Betty Friedan changes her mind and moves into "the second stage" of feminism (returning to family and winning male collaboration to build family, now that the damage is done.

There is a "moral majority" out there (meaning they want some of the right things for many wrong reasons). There also is something called "*her*pes (excuse our sexism—*his*pes, if you please).

The Department of Labor announces in the black press that while white women gained in terms of labor force participation during the 70s as blacks slipped back. We had predicted this in 1969 and proved it statistically by 1974.

57

The concept of "comparable pay" is enacted in San Jose and passes the San Francisco Board of Supervisors. Soon it will be advocated nationwide. In this little doozy, selected occupations traditionally woman will have salaries raised across the board to equal those deemed "comparable" to selected "men's" occupations. In effect, white women predominantly would have white clerical jobs raised to equal the pay for blue collar occupations comprising the major current ceiling for black males.

1982. The ERA fails to receive ratification when many previous backers, frightened that its vague language could usher in court demands that not only would prove bizarre, but also petty unisexual lingusitic changes in all would take away some of female privileges such as freedom from compulsory, heavy-duty, military service.

NOW vows to go after distractors and to unseat unfriendly politicians or any others who fail to bow to their ideals. The NAACP and other Jewish organizations adopt a similar policy for themselves.

An epidemic of genital herpes has swept the Western world. With sexual license goes certain side effects. The wages of sin is herpes.

A debilitating disease invades the homosexual communities in epidemic proportions. It is called "immuno-deficiency syndrome. According to the *New England Journal of Medicine,* study shows more than 80 percent of homosexual volunteers had far fewer white blood cells to fight infection when compared to a heterosexual control group.

Professor Geoffrey Thobrun and Dr. Richard Harding of Monash University inform the *Melbourne Age* newspaper there is no reason an embryo fertilized in laboratory could not be implanted in the belly of a man and derived later by Caesarian section. Prof. Carl Word, of Monarch Univerisity's test tube baby program, reports that embryos have already been successfully implanted in male mice. Do we

58

really need this one?

The United States and the World Bank are concerned that some nonwhite nations, Africans especially, have resisted their birth control programs, largely due to cultural factors. Fran Hosken, editor of *WIN* (Women's International Network) News, is policing black publications, threatening to persuade large white advertisers to pull out if they are not critical of African reproductive culture opposed by feminists. These same forces keep trying to persuade the Arabs to give up the veil. Fran Hoskens has even started urging the United States to withold aid from targeted African countries clinging to their own culture of reproduction.

One third of all U.S. foreign aid (more than $1 *billion* a year) now goes to Israel. Yet the black intellectual is effectively silenced by the Jewish-dominated publishing, film and media industries and by black intellectual opportunism and timidity. Accommodationism is in its apex. Even while foaming at the bits over the slightest hint of the idea of a black matriarchy (once a sociological figure of speech, a misnomer, for the broken patriarchy of the race), even black nationalist intellectuals in our day will assert the existence of matriarchies in ancient-Africa. They confuse matriarchal and matrilineal.

Other than in mythology, there is no anthropological evidence or other real-life record of the existence of a matriarchy (where women actually rule men) anywhere since the beginning of time. However, white feminists, re-writing and infusing even biology textbooks with these new fantasies, not to mention history, employ the smoke-screen that most anthropology (oh, Margaret Mead) has been written by men.

Black intellectuals in turn explain it has been written by whites, but even so, black intellectuals who profess to find matriarchies are merely accommodating to the white

59

feminist ideals and the white liberal agenda. In claiming to have orginated the idea of a matriarchy in ancient Africa, the black intellectuals are in effect out-doing, out-whiting the whites!

Not long ago, a nationalist-dominated group, enacted a rule that, henceforth and forevermore, one-half of its officeholders, come what may, will be women. Years ago, at a time when the white American Psychological Association was promoting the unisexual/feminist ideology and trying to elect its first woman president, the Association of Black Psychologists had quietly elected women, in one crescendo, to be concurrently its President, its Secretary, and its Treasurer. However, the black race will have no partriarch in a partriarchal land. The black race will outstrip the whites in the service of the white agenda.

Meanwhle, unhinged from its most legitimate historical spoke in the wheel of liberation, America is turning, floundering, to the Right. From the Afro-Americans, the only group brought here predominantly against its will, the one that gave birth to the blues, the white liberals have taken the blues and the revolutionary initiative and gone. Dominated by the white ethnics, children of European immigrants, white liberals are dragging the ambivalent WASPs and the silent "moral majority," on a tow-line to unisexualization.

Like rape, overwhemingly visited upon the black and the poor woman, abortion is being exploited by white feminists as a weapon in the power struggle between the Left and the Right. More quietly, a WASP-white ethnic divergence is being exploited to camouflage in the public mind the more gruesome elements of the unisexual program of population eugenics. Reagan speaks out against abortion, with a flair for the dramatic, but hedges and tosses the buck to others; so that, as of this writing, he has not actually endorsed one *anti*-abortion law.

Before Reagan, Nixon, no card-carrying feminist, cemented and gave clout and legitimacy, codification, federal financing and arms, to the forces of unisexualization. Jerry Ford remains snugly at home with his feminist wife, Betty Ford. Lady Bird Johnson has emerged from the closet of Southern comfort to coalesce with her daughter, Linda Robb; and there is peace in the Reagan family as his heart goes out to his feminist daughter, Maureen, who wishes to be more like dad (instead of mom) and his ballet-dancing son, perhaps the archetype of future inheritors of the White House throne.

Where is your family now?—and what is your family going to?

61

The Rise of Homosexuality and Diverse Alternatives to Matrimony

There are signs of the times. The economic structure is falling. Our psychical capacities are daily corroded and, with these things, our ability to contend and cope in a decaying and decadent society is all but paralyzed. Let us repent. The liberal-radical-moderate-establishment-coalition holds out tremulous solutions to our family disintegration that are not corrective but mere extensions of the problem. For instance, anti-male feminism, indeed, anti-maternal feminism, ultra-permissive childrearing, the romanticizing of single parenthood, unisexism and unisexualization.

Understand that we have not one modicum of opposition to such things as gay human rights or full equality and freedoms for everyone, including the right of women to exist with full equality as women without having first to become more and more like men. Similarly, there is nothing wrong with being a single parent, for instance, though everybody knows that parenting is hard enough for two or more these days. But there is something wrong with the fact that black women, through no real choice of their own, are more frequently relegated to that condition by comparison because of some other race's depletion of their male supply. Almost two out of five black females in this decade will never marry, including those who will long to do so.

Taken collectively, the above "solutions" will have the

sinister effect of further splintering or nuclearizing the family unit. They are but unconscious adaptations to the demands of post-industrial society. A presidential committee, moreover, has recommended that we let the cities die and that we foster and promote contrarily mass migration from region to region wherever the job market takes us. This kind of society, which we call cybernetic or post-industrial for want of a better name, will require inhabitants with increasingly superficial and tentative relationships to enable them to move wherever the economy shifts them. This is but a continuation to a final stage of what we have called mass urbanization.

The cybernetic society will demand, indeed is already producing, an ever more amorphous family system (let us call it the amoebic family) wherein ephemeral unions such as shacking are the norm, doing your own thing, and living to be by yourself. It is amoebic because it has no clear, permanent form, shape or fashion.

More consequential even than the cultivation of singleness is the production of unidimensional sexuality. Herbert Marcuse had seemed to anticipate much of this in his *One Dimensional Man* and *Eros and Civilization*. People traditionally debate whether homosexuality brought on the fall of Greece and Rome or not, when actually what happened was the diametric reverse. Whenever a society such as ancient Greece or the Western world of today is in a state of decay or long-term disarray, norms and values are confused and chaotic, and people are alienated and set apart from their natural origins, there emerges a breakdown in childrearing and socialization, the capacity to rear children and usher them into maturity. Without a solid core to their personalities, children will grow up confused and inclined to develop problems of identity, most notably that of gender confusion. Homosexuality accordingly will proliferate and, in turn, will feed upon the

64

unisexualized society and impact upon it in a vicious circle. An article in the American Journal of Psychotherapy has charted the particulars of the institutionalization of homosexuality in the United States and the Western World, laying bare and citing names and dates and places in the politics of the normalization of homosexuality that occurred in the 1970's so-called sexual revolution. But we do not need the American Journal of Psychotherapy to see that just as those black persons who disidentify with their race and long to alter their skin color and facial features to approximate that of the white race may be found to suffer a racial identity crisis, the homosexual individual who disidentifies with his/her biological body to the point of subjecting it to the surgery of sex-change operations similarly suffers a gender identity confusion, to say the least.

So we will not need to engage in endless debates about the pros and cons of homosexuality. We know that homosexuality does not promote black family stability and that it historically has been a product largely of the Europeanized society. On the other hand—and this is crucial—we will refuse to embark upon one more tangent of displaced contempt and misdirected scorn for the homosexualized black brother or sister or drive them over to the camp of the white liberal-radical-moderate-establishment-coalition. What we must do is offer the homosexual brother or sister a proper compassion and acceptance without advocacy. We might not advocate, for instance the religion of Mormonism, or venereal disease, laziness or gross obesity, but we would nevertheless not toss a brother or sister so characterized completely out of the family. Some of them may yet be saved. And yet, we must declare open warfare upon sources of our brother's and sister's confusion. The liberal-radical-moderate-establishment-coalition has even turned its attack upon the Boy Scouts of America. White teachers infiltrate black child centers, nurseries and primary schools, compelling black boys to play with blonde dolls in the name of progress; and they are determined to leave no path to a clear and coherent masculine indentity. In every way, unisexualization and homosexuality are lionized, produced, promoted and inevitable.

Within this state of unisexualism and family disintegration, "omnigamy" (wherein everybody is married to or takes up with just about everybody else at the same time), our intellectuals (who generally see nothing until it has already passed), are beginning to weep and worry about the dying nuclear family, seeking alternatives. Women are talking of giving up on the struggle completely—some through lesbian experimentation and others through compensatory celibacy and diverse forms of sexual anorexia. Many black males are looking towards polygamy, and its advocacy.

It is true that before the Europeanization of the world, polygamy had a decided and honorable place alongside monogamy, particularly in Ancient Africa. There is a book called Polygamy Reconsidered that spells out this all but hidden portion of our society's history. However, African polygamy was a complex means of family organization and procreation, and we must take pains to ensure that it does not in Afroamerica become a simple means of heightened sexual gratification. Thus the embryonic polygamy of today presents to us a difficult dilemma. Sisters who never fear or shun to expose themselves to exploitation by monogamous males, or by males in a state or situation of monogamy, will use the fear of exploitation as a basis for rejecting or opposing polygamous arrangements.

Accordingly, the advocates of polygamy are learning to point out that polygamy will not be for everybody and that some persons will continue to thrive in monogamous affairs while others begin to glory in polygamous unions. Too many brothers, however, lacking the routines and guidelines of an unbroken tradition and culture of polygamy, too quickly enter it by the back door. Rather than finding women who have/can realize the potential economic and collective benefits of polygamous arrangements and uniting with them in a bond of matrimony, too many brothers will enter a marriage then find themselves, after years of contractual monogamy, to be torn by a preference for polygamy. They then face the difficulties of persuading their monogamous mate to cross over to their way of thinking. Moreover, rather than taking up this challenge of advocacy and persuasion, at least with their own mate, before embarking upon a concrete application, they will tend to find themselves with a willing other woman and the grueling challenge of converting the monogamous wife. Thus the advocates of polygamy (or the more enlightened among them) are wise to quickly lay down the rule that the women must do the choosing of one another; not the brother.

So let us not be afraid to consider every alternative to our current plight. At this time, we will not be intimidated by rigid theoreticians on either side.

Any form of marriage must serve in part this traffic light function in order to curb man's desire for sexual variety in the interest of his and everybody's need for psychological and social stability.

History has shown us that the only real mistake that an oppressed individual or people can make is to do nothing to seek social change. Everything else is a part of the process of exhausting and eliminating the spurious and incorrect solutions so as ultimately to evolve and arrive at the correct solution and, in time, our freedom or whatever else we want.

Finally, whatever we do, we must endeavor to ensure that our approach, though appearing progressive and correct on the surface, does not amount in the end to a mere accommodation to the circumstances of today's systematic depletion of the black male supply. Instead we shall rise up to change our state to that befitting our ancestral ancient African kings and queens.

What Makes a Man a Pimp?

Street pimps are secretive of necessity, talking freely only to those they know or trust, resting by day and dressing by night in the more shady regions of the ghetto. Thus, to some people they represent cruel psychopathy and degradation, to others the apex of glamor and sexual manliness.

Although pimps make a conscious effort to convey a cold, hard attitude toward the world and its inhabitants, especially their women, they often are very human individuals, equipped with all the usual feelings and emotions. They live and abide by their own customs and codes of behavior, maintain their own strict hierarchy of prestige and status, and employ a vicious "mind game" to give warmth and support, as well as somtimes brutal treatment, to their women.

Pimps regard their profession as one of the most severe, nervewracking and complicated in the entire world and take considerable pride in assuming responsibility for the upkeep, the care and feeding of their families of origin and "in-laws" as well. Although they see themselves as somehow outside—and even in rebellion against—the general society, they long for public recognition and acceptance. "The secret dream of every pimp is one day to be a square," says Spellman Young, ex-pimp and now articulate drugabuse counselor in Chicago.

The mutual scorn and distrust between the public and the pimp-whore coterie divide them further and draw the pimps and whores closer together in a sub-culture of psycho-social support. The pimp, who feels he must dominate the prostitute, exploits this separation from the square world by employing some fundamental tactics of brainwashing to enforce a physical and social isolation of the whore from her family and former friends. In this way, he controls all social contacts and relationships, a situation often reinforced by the tendencies of relatives and old acquaintances to ostracize the whore. "Cutting her off from her family, the pimp makes her totally dependent on him and then totally destroys her ability to think for herself," says Spellman.

In the effort to rule by the mind game, the pimp employs a rather advanced technique of fractionalized abuse, the "kiss-and-kick" principle, in preference to a steady or unrelenting flow of harsh treatment. Criminology professor Wallace Sifford, of Laney College in Oakland, Calif., tells of a pimp who last year gave his stable a big Thanksgiving feast and the entire day off. Sweet Ernie Smith, who as a pimp supported his mother and a dozen younger siblings, recalls pimps who would baby-sit and serve as fathers to their whores' children by former mates and as stepsons to their mothers-in-law.

On the other hand, Iceberg Slim, who pimped in Cleveland, Detroit and the Chicago area, will never forget the often tragic consequences of playing the game. One of his whores, new to the stable and the most attractive of all, complained one night of not feeling very well. Not wishing to offend the rest of the stable by appearing to give her special treatment, Iceberg turned her back out into the street with a warning to "keep humping bitch." Finally, one of the other whores persuaded Iceberg that her complaining colleague was really ill. It was too late. She died of a ruptured appendix.

What makes a man a pimp?—To exploit and abuse a

woman for simple monetary gratification; to drive her into the streets to walk and wait in the cold, hard night or the heat of a nocturnal summer; to sell her body to strange and sometimes repulsive men while looking to him (the pimp) as her only man; to contact disease and sometimes to die? While almost all pimps have known and reflected the consequences of early poverty, racism and social rejection, they tend to list such factors as only three of the forces that push them into pimping—"street poisoning," as some call it. In a "predatory evironment" and "the culture of the street," they encounter older pimps as role models and mentors (Sweet Jones stands out in Iceberg's memory) who take them under their wings as errand boys in their 12 or 13-year-old innocence, impressing them with "compelling rainbow-colored stables" of womanhood, big cars, ready cash, fine clothes and the smell of sweet cologne, inspiring them with personal praise and predictions of their own future success: "That young dude's going to make him a lot of money; look at him." And the whores all laugh and echo the pimps.

However, the ease with which pimps and whores recruit young boys often is aided by the nature of the boy's relationship with and attitudes toward his parents and parental figures. Most attest to feelings of rejection by their mothers and tend to transfer their rage and hatred to other women in later life. "I've seen stellar fellows who have never known love and affection," says Iceberg Slim. He and Spellman Young, by contrast, felt "spoiled" by their mothers. "And yet," Iceberg reminisces today, "I lived in a pit of hate. My whole career as a pimp was a compulsive role replay dedicated to one thing, my mother. Though my mother had a heart of gold, I felt she was too possessive; but I knew she loved me. She never missed a night, until I was 16, coming into my bedroom and sitting down and saying something sweet and beautiful. She worried about me and was always holding me close and kissing me."

"As an only child I too was possessive and screened her affairs like a husband. One night she went out to a tavern. I followed her and found her and went in and told her I wanted her to come out of there." Years earlier, Iceberg's mother, who only late in life was able to find a mutually satisfying mate, had left Iceberg's revered stepfather (father to him) for a prettier, slicker man; and Iceberg never quite forgave her until too late. She died while he was still in prison.

This troubled pattern in mother-son relationships is corroborated by the observations of such black female scholars as Dr. Ruth King, national president of the Association of Black Psychologists, and Elsie Cross, chairperson of the National Training Laboratory Institute near Washington, D.C., and herself a mother who fears that pimping may grow too popular.

Sweet Ernie Smith grew up in the Los Angeles home of a devoted mother, a high-school graduate, and a hardworking father, who had only completed the third grade but who worked overtime to keep his wife in the role of housewife and mother. Sweet Ernie came into conflict with his father when he took the side of school authorities who had tested Ernie and declared him in the subnormal range, particularly in verbal facility (Erinie is now a Ph.D in linguistics).

Ernie's family had migrated from Oklahoma, which helped lead him to experience a conflict of cultures. He began to feel that his own efforts to adjust, as he bounced from "dumb-boy" classes to schools for the incorrigible, were succeeding no better than those of his father. If the roof sprang a leak, his mother might tell his father that "any real man would go to the landlord and make him fix this roof." If his father went to the landlord, then got into an argument, the family would be forced to move, posing a setback in wages and other expenditures. If the f placed his rage in violence toward his wife, the polic is, "the man") would be called and his father would ╮ jailed, losing wages and bail money too. Sweet Ernie decided that he didn't want to be that kind of man, and, in his negative identity with his father ("I couldn't identity with him and his lunchbox life and his coping strategy of taking low") he soon fell into association with a pimp callled "School Boy," a semiliterate migrant from Tennessee who was always advising, "Get you some edjumacation." At 17, Sweet Ernie was driving a Cadillac.

Looking back now from the halls of higher learning, Dr. Sweet Ernie Smith recalls how he also came to scorn other father figures (male school-teachers, probation officers, and social workers) as "black men with peckerwood noses coming out of their heads." He watched their bourgeois approach to women with a curious contempt: "Hello darling, gee, your attire, that's certainly a lovely dress, and your hair style is simply gorgeous. You're certainly provocative." Later, he would listen to some pimp appproach a strange woman: "Hey, Mamma, you know who this is? I'm Pretty Eddy, the best thing that happened to a woman since panty hose. Honey, you choose me, all you got to do is bathe in milk, fast through silk, and sleep under satin quilts." Or: "Bitch, congratulations! I'm going to make you a superstar." Mostly what you're telling the girl is how exciting you're going to make her life," Sweet Ernie explains.

"Everybody wants to be a star," Iceberg Slim notes. "If a whore can say 'I'm Pretty Slim's woman,' she can bask in his reflected glory." Coming from a poor and often a broken home, and without exceptional talents to market in legitimate society, she can seldom expect to make it to routine stardom. Her association with the pimp satisfies her womanly longing to be attached to a man of power and stature. The pimp's conspicuous display, dazzl-

73

ing in its splendor, attracts and intrigues her--his late-model, gold-plated Cadillac, his ready cash, his reputation, her furs (if she is lucky), and their diamond rings. These are items of value which, particularly in the low-income section of the ghetto, constitute flashy, portable signs of affluence which are, at the same time, more easily acquired, hot or cold, than some more stable and actually more expensive items, such as a modest house or a small but comfortable business.

Beyond such symbols of affluence, according to San Francisco psychologist Thomas Hilliard, the pimp provides the whore with somebody strong to lean on and, in the snarls and snares of the universe, somebody to show her the way. Dr. Hilliard points out that some black women, recoiling against the stereotypes of the strong black woman, fear being thought unfeminine. The strong man makes them feel more like a woman, reinforces their basic femininity. The pimp, accordingly, reaps a paradox of scorn and shadowy prestige in the love life of the streets. "To some women, the pimp is the epitome of masculine appeal," testifies Valerie Troutt, the Educational Director of C.H.A.N.G.E., a black mental health facility in Berkeley.

Thus, a preoccupation with personality as a weapon of love pervades the psychological modalities of the street pimp, manifesting itself typically in a constant endeavor to affect a narcissistic (self-loving) peacock demeanor in interactions with his women. Much of this behavioral style spills over into the mannerisms of men who would be pimps but in fact are not, and, along with the general motivation of the pimp, constitutes a rebellion against a thwarted masculinity—a redefinition of manliness and sex roles, according to Sweet Ernie. "A man don't wear pink clothes. A black player can. A man don't wear lime and loud yellow and beige. . A black player can. A man don't get his fingernails polished and toenails manicured. A black player can.

74

A pimp takes on the most effeminate things and makes them masculine."

However, "most pimps are lousy lovers," Iceberg Slim concedes, and contrary to popular belief, the basic attraction between pimp and whore is not a sexual one. "I acted like I was Apollo, but pimping is not a beauty contest," Iceberg says. "The pimp has to be cold, stay in cold storage. I'd lay in bed with my surrogate lover (many pimps keep Teddy Bears and the like in their bedrooms), pretending not to want some fine brown frame. 'You sure got a one-track mind, woman. Hurry up!' " In the end, however, a woman is said to place less value on sex by comparison and is able eventually to turn the tables on a man. At the same time, says Spellman Young, "the whore retains her ability to make money long after the pimp loses his."

The tragedy of a pimp's life is that he confuses domination with genuine strength, focusing on a push-button psychology (the mind-game) in his relations with women and effecting a kind of backfire-ridden psychical slavery. "The square wants to make a sexual conquest," Iceberg explains. "The pimp wants to make a total conquest." To do so he must sometimes resort to cruelty and misuse, even mayhem and violent abuse, but all the time, says Iceberg, "the whore is stacking her cards and her constant secret dream is someday to bankrupt the pimp." Iceberg will admit that, in all his years as a pimp, he never fully managed to understand the "gamemanship of the female." "If I had, I never would have wound up in the penetentiary." While Iceberg was in the pen the last time, his "bottom woman" (main whore) of 13 years left for another man, to whom she gave Iceberg's car and other possessions—even his dog.

According to Spellman Young, the pimps have an axiom that in the end the game turns around, leaving too many pimps as defeated dope addicts, or in the penetentiary, or wandering meaninglessly, now shabbily dressed and deteriorated, up and down now dreary ghetto streets and in and out of cheap barrooms, boasting to sustain their pride and trying to call back in conversation the youth and capacities that have gone forever.

"But it's justice," says Iceberg Slim, who served four terms in the penetentiary but somehow got out of pimping in time. "Any man who can handle a dozen women has no business being a pimp in the first place."

The Pimp-Whore Complex:
Learning to Love/Hate

The dehumanization of the oppressed, wrote Frantz Fanon, is a prerequisite to effective colonization and human subjugation. This dehumanization exhibits its most devastating and conspicuous features in the case of relations between the oppressed male and female, who comprise the basis for the family unit in the colonized society. In the process of destructuring male-female relations, the ability to love or to feel loved is decimated. We shall see that this fact was borne out by our sample, but first it is necessary to discuss briefly the relevant psychological aspects of the phenomenon called love.

To begin with, according to Theodore Reik, love is cultural and learned and necessitates self-love which in turn grows out of the expectation that the individual will be loved. "This 'self-love' which is really the love of someone else for oneself is thus a late, secondary formation like pity, which also unconsciously presupposes the pity of one's mother or another dear person for oneself—more than that, our self-love will remain dependent on others, and will always be the unconscious anticipation of this admiration or appreciation . . .Thus behind self-love is the unconscious knowledge that the person is or will be loved."

Reik contrasts this view with the ideas which Freud's followers present. Such thinkers believe that an individual's capacity for loving is "restrained by narcissism, this self-love, that a person who loves himself too much cannot love others." Reik maintained that there is no original and genuine self-love and that "one's ability to love is impaired by lack of self-confidence by self-dislike or self-contempt and by too little self-love, that most of he emotional difficulties which we have with others are mere reflections and manifestations of the conflicts that we have with ourselves." Anna Freud has referred to the "turning of aggression against the self" as a defense mechanism employed by the ego in response to conflict generated by the internalization of external sources of self-esteem or inferiority. That the opressed internalize the attitudes of the oppressors toward themselves, the oppressed, is now well known.

This feeling of self-love is distorted, in a collective sense and frequently individually, for blacks living under color oppression. If love, unlike sex, according to Reik, is a very definite relationship between a me and a you, the black individual might find it easy enough to love but more difficult to feel loved, in that the black "I" does not love the black "me." This predicament is not remedied by a feeling of sexual attraction which may often be pursued as a substitute for the love that is otherwise missed. Hence black males and females in our study tended to emphasize satisfaction with their sex lives and the sexual aspect of their mates as over against the love or social relationship. Indeed, the sexual attractiveness of the mate may merely aggravate the jealousy arising from the difficulties of feeling loved. It is necessary to distinguish between the self and the social self and in turn the sexual self. This consideration will reappear later.

A content analysis of our study of the self concepts and sexual images of black males and females confirms the foregoing difficulties of loving, the collective nature of black intersexual conflicts, and our general thesis of the relative oppression of the black male as a primary factor in black male-female relations. Although individual self esteem may confict with the image one holds of persons possessing similar social characteristics, the way in which the self image and the social self of black males and females differ is instructive for our hypothesis.

Respondents were asked to describe by turn the typical black male, the typical black female, the typical white male, the typical white female, your mate and yourself. Out of their responses emerged the fact, supported by casual observation in everyday life, that when black males criticize black females, it is typically for being too strong, independent and aggressive. But when black females criticize black males, it is for being too weak and inadequate in the masculine arena. On an individual plane this is true for any race, including whites, as in both instances such criticism suggests that the individual condemned is in violation of the socially approved sexual norms and expectations. But that is just the point: in the black race the criticism is collective and identifies that fact that neither black males nor females have been permitted to fully play the sexual roles that are socially ascribed. Simultaneous with the much discussed emasculation of the black male came the defeminization of the black woman.

The fact nevertheless remains that the female's image is one of strength while the male's is one of weakness. To some extent of course we are dealing with stereotypes, but stereotypes have a way of being based on a certain reality or at least to emerge as a self-fulfilling prophecy which is self-generating and self-sustaining. In the case of the black male and female, however, a stereotype can be said to comprise only a part of the picture.

When asked to describe the typical black male, all but one of the female respondents produced a negative concept. The middle class criticism revolved around a picture of the black male as a failure in the masculine role, while the lower class women, though concerned with his lack of financial support, lay stress on a perceived black male mistreatment of black women in terms of physical and emotional abuse. The black male corroborates these views of himself, bemoaning his own defeatism and familial malingering and viewing the white man as more positive in familial support and achievement. The black female by contrast detests and shuns the white male. Thus the black male's concept of the white male is more favorable than the black female's. The lower class black male likewise is dissatisfied with the work history of the typical black male and sees the ideal male as hard working and supportive of his family. This is only one indication that he accepts the values pertaining to the male role in this society but somehow is thwarted in the performance of that role. The ideal male not only is respectful of his woman and attentive to her, he also may be engaged in civil rights activism and other humanistic pursuits. Most black women, while acknowledging the desirability of such traits as humanistic endeavor and even economic productivity, emphasize the value of the male's interpersonal relations and treatment of women as wives and lovers.

By comparison with the black female, as we shall see, the black male is thought to fall short of the ideal expectations. This is not only true for the black female's conception of the black male but also for the black male's concept of himself, the black male. Thus the black male does not manage to approximate his own ego ideal. The black male may even be seen as a human facade, devoid of the social essence and characterological attributes of manliness. In describing the typical black male, one lower class female respondent replied:

"To me the typical black man is a difference to me in a man and just a person with man features. Because a real man is going to be a real man at all times. He's going to learn to respect the woman he is with and do right by her at all times. He's gonna try not to hurt her in any kind of way if he loves this woman. He's gonna do things that are very pleasing to her as long as she's doing right by him. Now just a man with a man features—it's a difference between a person who's actually a man and a person who calls himself a man and a person that has man's features. In the other person who isn't a man in manly ways is gonna disrespect his woman. He doesn't care about her feelings one way or the other. He's just sort of doing whatever he feels like doing regardless, whether who gets hurt. I can only put it that way—the two differences."

While most black males and females attest to the special impact of oppression on the black male, they differ in that the black male repsondents stress their necessity for compensatory behavior of a pathological sort while the black female bemoans a perceived sense of defeatism in the black male. She may feel that the black male rightfully sees his position in society as problematic and "downright dangerous," but that he too often is inclined to blame all of his failures on his blackness. They are seen as discouraged and demoralized and living afraid of failures, beaten down by a combination of oppression and their own response to it. The white male is thought to care more for his women. Lower class respondent: "They love them better. They can give them more. They don't have to be so contankerous because they've always had control over their women. They don't fight their women as much." Or: "The white man will go to any length to help his family, will do anything to make his family happy. But the black man wants something for nothing, wants it all for himself instead of his family. It is not in the black man to want what I want—to settle down and have a home and have children—I don't know why." Comments from the middle class: "Black men are immature and childish, no matter how old they are. They're looking for another mother when they grow up. I don't care about getting married again because I don't want to raise another boy. You constantly have to build them up to keep them going."

But a lower class black male expained it this way:

"The black man wants to strike out, but most of the time his woman can't back him up. He's always put in the boy position. Say the woman gets $100 more a month. That makes him have to go to her—not in all cases but in too many cases. The white world's still got us more or less in the boy position. Half the things black men do wrong are due to their oppression." Or: "The black man sees himself as unsuccessful because of the obstacles placed in his way by white society. He see his woman as seeing him unsuccessful because of his own inadequacy."

Black males almost unanimously see the hardest thing about being a black man as revolving around economic and occupational problems—that is, making it in the system. They see the problem as the system of white exploitation. The black female, while also recognizing the sociogenic hardships of being a black woman in this society, is almost unanimously inclined to relate her main difficulty to her compensation for the failure of the black male. She sees her problem as the black man—her need to help him, his tendency to leave her alone with the children, and the demands of compensation for the loss of a husband or a father or both. Denied authority socio-politically and individually, the black male may feel impelled to overcompensate for this emasculation by becoming ultra chauvinistic. Such men are "caught up in trying to prove that they're a man—to the black woman, to the white man, and to himself."

Although some black female respondents described their

mates as desirable in the sense that they were warm, intelligent and a good lover, ambitious and successful, almost ideal, most saw them as reluctant to work, irresponsible and generally unable to cope or play an acceptable male role. In addition, they were not infrequently seen as possessive and jealous or otherwise "hard to live with."

By contrast, black male respondents often described their mates as ideal women. But they were equally as likely to describe them as domineering and controlling. In fact, such conflicts in power relations were the only negative evaluations indicated, all other characterizations being positive when black male respondents described their mates. The black males typcially looked up to black females as a group and many feel that the black male is somewhat dependent on the black female for social and psychological support. At the same time the black female longs for a strong black man to lean on and expresses the need for his collaboration. However, she feels that the strong black male either eludes her or/and exists in rare abundance. In any case, this dependence on her man, which increasingly in the present day is scorned by the white woman, has historically been denied the black woman. The black female's concept of an ideal female is not the strong, domineering type she believes black women or herself to be, although she is able to have pride in her strength. However, she does not like this role that white society has placed upon her—a role combining some of the traditional demands of the male and female roles.

The black male concedes the validity of the popular image of the black female's strength. However, he may see this as excessive in that she is domineering, "pushy," even "castrating." He regrets her dissatisfaction with the black male but appreciates the fact that many are "understanding" of his condition. Some see the salient feature of the black female to be her sex appeal while others regard her as opportunistic and materialistic. The white woman is equally as likely to be seen as materialistic and opportunistic, but is characteristically thought to be more understanding, self-sacrificing and supportive by comparison. Nevertheless, she is deplored by some as racist and hostile, and there is a general preference for the black woman's relative ability to relate to black consciousness and black culture.

The black male believes that what's good about the black female is her strength and her ability to deal with oppression and the vicissitudes of her family. To some degree, he also believes that the black woman understands him better than the white woman does, is able to manage his wounded ego better and "won't let you cry."

> "What's good about the black woman? She's the backbone of the black man. You know, she has the initiative to do something about herself. She's really the backbone. A lot of the brothers think when you say the black woman is the black man's back bone, he feels there is a deficiency in him but it's not. She's his helpmate. She's his initiative, his strength. You know, when he feels down and out. I know it works with me. When I feel down and out and depressed, I don't go to no psychiatrist; I go to my woman."

Thus the black woman is honored for her strength and support. The black female admires the black male for his sexual qualities and his sex appeal. Otherwise she has only criticisms to make because of his neglect of the family, his mistreatment of the black female, in her view, or his alleged attraction to the white female. However, there is some tribute paid to his stamina in the face of the tremendous social obstacles confronting him.

Predictably, the black female admires her qualities of strength and independence, while the black male is vague or ambiguous in describing any good qualities the black male

84

might possess. He is quicker to acknowledge a black male dependency on the black female.

"She knows what you have been through and what you are going through and is just able to understand. But yet she won't let you cry. Won't let you take the easy way out. Like I know my mother a many a day my father would be drunk and mother would make him get up and go to work before she left. And if he had his way, I think he would forget work. But my mother, she told him, you know, you must go."

While the black female is inclined to discount the existence of an ideal mate, the black male readily regards the ideal black female as supportive psychologically and politically, as sharing the same values. She is not to be domineering or castrating but rather feminine and gentle, and yet it is sometimes desirable that she be strong and supportive. Thus the black male must yield to his ambivalence in the conflict between subjective perference and situational demands. This ambivalence is often reflected by the black female, who overwhelmingly regards the ideal female as understanding and respectful of her mate, supportive and patient, strong and devoted to her family, while remaining or often feigning femininity and dependence. She too sees the typical black female as strong and in some ways superior, necessitating her role as the backbone of the black family and the socio-economic supplement of the black male.

Sometimes this leads to a psychosocial fusion in which she regards herself as a role duality—a father and a mother, a male and a female, literally assuming the male role. Asked to describe herself, no. 0035 replied:

"I don't know. I'm not a great housekeeper . . . a lot of things you would think a man would do, paint, I do the painting. And I'm able to work on an occasional problem of my car. When something breaks down, I'm always there with a screwdriver to fix it. So I try a lot of things. I was by myself for a while. I didn't have no man around. So I had to do it by myself. Still, when my husband's around he doesn't do a lot of things—I have to do them. I don't know. I wouldn't say I'm perfect, but I try my best."

The black female may not only be perceived as stronger than the black male: "some are men in respects." Or: "The black woman has a hard time being a wife to a man; she tends to become the mother." Others may constantly strive to humiliate the black man. One told of feeling powerful and in control whenever she could make a man experience an orgasm while she did not.

Some attribute the black female's independence to a generational transmission of intersexual style and set of values. No. 0018F, who has a master's degree but is married to a man who did not attend college, put it this way:

"I'm not saying this right, but I think we are aggressive and dominating and domineering. But I think it's because we've had to be. Like our mothers before us and our grandmothers and great-grandmothers had to. You pick up from them. Cause mothers tell their daughters: You know he's not going to be able to support you, and you're going to go and have to get you an education and help him. And you know you gonna have to do this and you know you gonna have to do that. Cause you know how these men are."

Thus the black woman is trained to be independent and make it on her own (often given the educational advantage), while the white woman by comparison is geared more to the expectation of acquiring masculine support. It is in this regard that the black female can feel superior to the white woman and does. " . . . black women have always

86

considered themselves superior to the white women . . . Black women have been able to envy white women (their looks, their easy life, the attention they seem to get from their men); they could fear them (for the economic control they have had over black women's lives) but black women have found it impossible to respect white women: I mean they never had what black men have had for white men, a feeling of awe at their accomplishments."

Although the black females in our sample resent the white female's pedestal in one sense, they took consolation in the fact that being placed on a pedestal has left the white female weak and gullible, groveling to men, particularly whenever she takes up with the black males in pursuit of the savage taboo and the superstud, as they frequently described it. At the same time, the white woman is thought to be rather morally depraved and sexually perverted while the black woman is believed to be strong and respectful of her female virtues. She is likely to hold contempt for the white female, regarding her as pampered and emaciated by her position on the sexual pedestal, presenting a submissive front to men while in reality she is believed evil, vicious and cunning. Thus the black female is more contemptuous of both the white female and the white male than is the black male. In describing themselves as individuals, black females most often conceived of themselves in a favorable light—affectionate and sexually competent, intelligent, or even a good cook. They typically adhered to traditional values of femininity, and, even when expressing negative conceptions of themselves, tended to acknowledge black male criticism—i.e., "I'm too domineering" or "bitchy." Some felt depressed, frustrated, nervous and insecure without a satisfactory mate, or unattractive. One indicated that she has now been driven to violence with the men in her life.

The black male respondents almost unanimously complain that the the primary problem in getting along with a black woman revolves around the sexual power struggle, particularly decision-making and the black man's job and career activities. He feels obstructed in the effort to be "his own man," to take business and financial risks, feels pressured and excessively criticized for his failures while pushed toward a nine-to-five employment pattern. In addition, the black woman may use sex as a weapon in her efforts to force him to comply or to please her and many lack resepct for him. Here the black female respondents generally confirmed the view of the black males.

In depicting her own difficulties in getting along with the black male on the other hand, the black female respondents voiced complaints largely centering on the black male's inability to accomplish their masculine ideals. He is too weak and unaggressive, unsuccessful and undependable in matters of finance and unable to "carry his load." He feels beaten down by the system and his negative self feelings, by his sense of failure, and he is inclined to bring his frustrations home. There he unwraps his sensitive and fragile ego and feels threatened by his mate. At the same time he fears being close to her, often exhibits hostility as a defense, and disdains to communicate and talk out problems with her. His unwarranted jealousy may give rise to fighting or cathartic violence. The black male concedes to feelings of inadequacy and defeatism but gives priority as a problem in the conflict to the fighting and violence that may have grown out of the dilemma of wanting to reign supreme in the relationship according to society's decrees while being impelled to look up to the black female.

Thus, "for the duration of their lives, many black women must bear a heavy burden of male frustration and rage through physical abuse, desertions, rejection of their femininity and general appearance. Having a job provides relief for her stomach but not for her soul, for a black woman's successful coping with the economic problem (and we might throw in the education problem) enhances her rejection by black men, or else invites acceptance in the form of exploitation. Stymied in his attempt to protect and free the black woman (and himself), the black man further degrades her. She, doubly powerless and vengeful, insults his manhood by whatever means at her disposal. Thus are many black men and women hateful partners in a harrowing dance."

The black male is believed to be resistant to thwarted masculine identities and a concomitant fear of femininity which leads him, the black female complains, to a significant disdain for tenderness. This lack of tenderness may take two forms—a propensity for violence and a disdain for interpersonal communication. This problem of communication has been documented, for instance, by Blood and Wolfe in a study of *"Negro-White Differences in Blue Collar Marriages in a Northern Metropolis."* Our study coroborated this finding for both middle and lower classes. However, neither black wives nor black husbands are as likely as whites to tell their spouses about their troubles after a bad day, for instance.

This low level of communication is doubly significant because of the necessity for black men to rely more on their personalities to compensate for inferior status and to achieve distinction in the black world. Add to this its importance as a criterion of mate selection by the black female. Nevertheless, the ability to command love or respect from a woman may depend more on power and social status than on personal or physical qualities. However, inasmuch as the black male is blocked from sources of power and social status, the black female will be moved to see the good qualities of the black male as centering on the compensatory characteristics of personal and sexual charm. For the black male, sexual prowess "has often been the means by which he has asserted and attained his masculinity." Contrarily the black male's admiration for the black woman does not give priority to her feminine (sexual object) qualities. This is in spite of the fact that the black woman historically "has been defined mainly as a sexual object . . ." and it is further documentation for the fact that along with the emasculation of the black male went the defeminization of the black female.

Nor is the importance of compensatory sexuality alien to an intrapsychic or psychoanalytic interpretation. Brenner has suggested that "to the slightly older child the penis and its activity is used, or at least conceived of (used in fantasy) as a weapon and a means of destruction respectively." Analysis has further shown that weapons used in games and fantasies involving spears, arrows, guns, etc. may represent the penis in unconscous thought. "It appears, therefore, that in his fantasies, he is unconsciously destroying his enemies with his powerful and dangerous penis." This possibility is widely acknowledged by black men who purport to "get back at the white man" in their sexual encounters with the white woman; and a black rapist may see his act as insurrectionary. However, the importance of sex as a weapon in the black male's quest for psychosocial masculinity may have its strongest realization in his relations with the black female.

But if the black male is denied institutionalized social and political instruments of masculinity and is impelled to compensate through sexual attraction and related activities, the black female similarly is forced to regard these compensatory masculine traits more highly than otherwise would be the case. Thus, while recognizing herself as aggressive, she may shun men who permit her to dominate them. No. 0021F: "I just don't like somebody that I can manipulate. I want somebody who has some backbone. Nobody likes a sponge." Or: no. 0038F: "I don't want him too nice cause I'd be testing him a lot. And just nice, so I could deal with him. Cause I can't deal with a too nice man. A nice man, that really upsets me. I mean a really, real nice man." Similarly, the black female may come to value the sexual because of its relative prominence as an asset among her source of males.

The Successful Black Woman's Man Problem

Where do we begin to tell the story of the heartache and the suffering that can sometimes derive from the conflict, cutting against the grain of patriarchy, between the black woman who feels that she is on the way up in the economic world and the black male who may, for whatever reason at any given moment, find himself still faltering along the way?

In the past their struggle has been mislabeled one between the "black matriarchy" and, more recently, "the black macho," when in reality, as we now know, the black macho is not the ultimate oppressor of the black woman, just as the black matriarch was not the oppressor of the black man. But there is a thing going on between them, between these two symbolic strains, which we should come to know more about although decidedly by some less malignant names. Once the black male and the black female have begun to better understand the fact that they exist under a common oppression, in all its myriad manifestations, they can move on to halt their currently excessive displacement of their rage onto one another. From there they may go on to heal the broken spirit of a noble race.

Not that there are no other potential allies. It is only that we, black men and women, are held together by a biohistorical imperative. The future of the black female is accordingly with the black male, just as the future of the black male must be with the black female. The white female also attests to a common oppressor, but the white woman sleeps with her enemy. For better or worse, we must never forget, her oppressor is her father, her son, her husband, her lover; and they are bound by the umbilical cord of biology itself.

Why then does there arise, between the black male and black female, such intensive and complex psychological warfare? Why does the black male so often feel so deeply threatened by a successful black female? The answers to these questions are as crucial as those to the sources of the much discussed but not fully understood attraction between the white female and the black male; and these are connected, for they are tied to the very essence of femininity and masculinity, orchestrated moreover by the black condition.

It isn't anybody's fault (outside of the economics of oppression and the institutional genocide, the social decay, of an over-industralized society), but the fact remains that the successful black woman's plight is magnified by the fact that she must marry beneath her station in life more often even than a successful man ordinarily would. This sets up an intricate and punishing set of intrapsychic problems (by now of course we are including in "marriage" any continual commitment involving a common abode, with or without a marriage license). This predicament appears to manifest itself more stringently the harder she tries to adapt to her society; for instance, she is more likely to marry than the successful white female, but she also is more destined to see her marriage fall apart. She has a higher number of years of school completed but the higher her education the less the supplement to her income derived from her mate. She even has fewer children, postponing immediate gratification perhaps too well, but the more children she has the more her marriage is going to be broken.

94

For she will find that it takes two to tango and that, in the struggle to synchronize her career and her mating, she is one of a few within the human race that is not so given to the art of role playing. Cunning white females will think nothing of playing one role on the job and another wholly different after five. For historically her worlds have been more spearate. The black woman, who long has had to be too often both mother and father to her family, goes into the marketplace more out of a sense of necessity. She leaves behind a portion of her heart and her interest there, her sense of self-importance, when she goes home; and this plays a heavy part in her overall life and her emotionality. The white woman's involvement in the marketplace (despite the rhetoric of the vocal feminists seeking unconsciously to rationalize the demands for two incomes within today's economy) is comparatively more of a luxury. She goes into the market place to find her self-identity, or she wishes to learn to feel a higher sense of self-worth, but her heart is in the home, the place that historically has been her haven.

Our studies show that the black woman is proud of her strength, of her historical resolve and resiliency in the service of her family, wherein she frequently had to leave the home or otherwise to be "the backbone" in her many times of storm. But, in her relations with her man, she fears that this very strength, imposed upon her unsolicited will someday be the death of her. She would give her right arm instead to have a strong black man to stand beside her, but she knows from observation and past experience that these are currently in short supply. The black male too is a secret admirer of the black woman's strength; and he will privately tell an inquiring stranger that he is grateful for her tenacity, that she is still his woman. He will testify that she has been a shelter, a steady leaning post. He will confess that he knows, deep down, that he's got a good woman, and he will say all the grateful things he may frequently find hard to express to her. In secret, he looks up to the black woman, admires her strength, but he also fears and resents it. Part of this resentment grows out of patriarchal norms and values, but also emanates from the fact that the woman he loves in adult life, his consummated lover, the one in a sense he has been preparing all of his life to meet, is of the exact same sex as was his mother. Thus many of his unresolved conflicts with his mother (who once kept his hand out of the cookie jar, extending and withholding pleasure will now be fought out with his mate. This is true of course to some degree of any male, but because the black mother is so often in effect both mother and father, an attitudinal set evolves in greater degree between the black man and the black woman as they grow into adulthood, and this is transmitted from one generation to the next through the cake of culture. Moreover, it is fanned, inflamed and distorted, by white standards of judging each other and the notions so well internalized from white racism and the white feminist agenda. This is not to say that there is not much that is very good in their relationship, but not without the ambivalence that derives directly from their social situation.

For her part, there is within the aggressive woman this longing to subdue a man, but once having succeeded, losing interest in him. A hardened man came into treatment one day crying, threatening suicide if his wife didn't take him back. The more he pleaded, whipped down by his past misconduct, the more she evaded him. Unknown to him his wife was saying that she likes a man who dominates her and that her new boyfriend dominates her. Psychoanalysts have even claimed to find what they call a "feminine masochism" among peasant women, and there is the notion in ghetto streets that many women don't feel right "unless they're getting their so-and-so's kicked sometimes." And it is true that many a woman has learned as a child, watching her mother's stormy love life, that a love that is deep is never still. Within the repertoire of the street pimp, in fact, is the almost routine adoption of the "kick-kiss" principle wherein he alternates a mean mistreatment and a syrupy sweetness as part of his "mind game" machinations. On the wall of the black cultural center at the University of Washington is an all-engulfing, painted mural of a black woman accompanied only by the words: "bearer of pain."

Without a strong black male, many would now agree, there can be no strong black race in a patriarchal society. The black woman has always known this on some innate level; but because she is not a social analyst, she is inclined to infantilize the black male, perhaps too readily enternalilizing white society's denigration of him, and she believes perhaps correctly that it is time now for the black male to make a change, to "clean up his act." She will accordingly wish too often to play holy mother, to concretize the goodness of the pseudomythological "strong black woman" to herself as an individual while incorporating her individual black mate into a generalized category of naughty infant. The black woman and the black man thus encounter each other with two contrary images of themselves and each other, expecting the worst, as naughty infant and punitive mother. Increasingly they will feel that aside from their own perspective, there is no other story to be told.

Though low income women complain more about problems in their treatment by their mates, black women of all classes tend more to emphasize satisfaction in their sexual relations and dissatisfaction in their interpersonal relations with their mates. The reason is that most black persons are not far removed in time and association from the low income strata, so that it is true that much of what is frequently described as black is really a characteristic of the low income strata at the same time as it is also true that what is true of the lower strata in extreme degree denotes a quality or flavor that permeates the oppressed black condition. It is a matter of degree. Such an instance, as we shall see, is what we may call "the Superfly syndrome."

Although Superfly embodies what we are calling the Superfly syndrome, he is only one manifestation; for it includes a broad range of young black males who, blocked from the avenues to social potency, overcompensate and conspicuously cultivate the ability to control and dominate females and their sexual relationships. The syndrome is not restricted merely to individuals who adopt the clothes and mannerisms reminiscient of the movie screen hero, Superfly, or the hep cat or jitterbug of yesteryear. The Superfly syndrome is as prevalent as the Superfly character in pure array is rare. While it is true that whites have Don Juan and Rudolph Valentino, neither achieved the stature of a collective social type in the manner of the ghetto's Superfly, neither was as pervasive. The Superfly syndrome derives quite understandably from the young black male's uncertainty about his adult role within the experience of a broken patriarchy (whether or not he has a broken home). If the young boy's father has not played his fatherly role sufficiently in accord with his normative expectations, the boy may fail to make the proper identification. Thus the Superfly syndrome grows out of the social situation of oppression, is learned or acquired; but the young black male may also take it as a model in compensation for the disillusionment he feels for institutionalized norms of masculinity to which his access is restricted. Studies show the young black male, for instance, exhibiting a higher level of heterosexual interaction at adolescence at the same time as his disdain for marriage increases with his age and emerging recognition of marriage as stymied by his relative access to occupational and economic life-chances. The compensatory valuation of superstud aspects of the masculine roles comes fully into view. Ironically, if not paradoxically, this character type, though based on a supersexist approach to women and sometimes a pathological hatred, is an attractive type among many young ghetto women. This attraction for the wayward male is also present among white women, and is thought to be fairly universal, but it is nowhere so pervasive and admired as within the urban black ghetto where it is a product of the low level of male attainment in the more conventional socio-economic aspects of manhood and society.

Within the adolescent culture of the urban ghetto, the Superfly character type is the most conspicuous male ideal. He possesses or strives to exhibit a possession of a "bad" personality, a super-ability to rap, "walking mean, looking clean attitude," to strut, and "get over" with whatever he may variously call a young woman. He longs for the flashy clothes, the big new car and ready cash his mentors appear to derive from the alternative economy of the ghetto. Above all, he stresses the importance of controlling the women in his life. For the pimp (the epitome of the Superfly caricature of the ghetto male's psycho-socio-sexual-style), this ability to manage women becomes his livelihood. The pimp has simply reversed the traditional roles of men and women, the roles too often denied him. He will reject those roles that reject him. He will be kept like a woman. He is kept by the woman. He is the pretty one, the prized sex object who uses sex as a weapon of love. By Superfly, we mean to capture something of that flavor but we also mean to encompass a wide range of specific types beside the pimp—the jitterbug, the street nigger, cool breeze, as well as the fainter strains that rub off on even many square black middle class males' personalities. The pimp-whore liason merely represents the caricature of a very real social phenomenon.

The pimp, the Superfly, is merely a pathetic social parody of a feminine abuse played out by men without social power, men who feel impelled to derive their sense of power and importance in their relationships with their women, almost exclusively within the sexual encounter. So it is that, faced with the enduring hardships of the Superfly syndrome, many women ambivalently relinquish altogether the struggle to be a desired sex object and to experience social harmony and socio-sexual satisfaction with men. They exhibit a kind of sexual anorexia. According to Grier and Cobbs in *Black Rage:* " . . . it may be that after a brief struggle a black woman feels that feminity, as it is defined in these times, is something she cannot achieve. Rather than having her heart broken every day, she relinquishes the struggle and diverts her interest elsewhere. She has denied some of the intensely personal satisfaction she might have received as an honored and desirable sex object." In so doing, she accomodates to the reality of the broken patriarchy which the successful black male is in a position to exploit. It is not surprising, therefore, that despite her conscious rejection of the Superfly as a cultural ideal, the black female is not infrequently drawn to him, finds him curiously attractive, interesting, and she will often unconsciously collaborate in "spoiling" and priming her own sons for the Superfly role out of fear that their manhood will be crippled. "Look at 'em," the proud old folks will say of the little boy. "He's going to be a heartbreaker." And they all laugh and think that it is good.

As middle class black women grow into maturity, they tend to turn their attention toward more mobile and therefore more conventional black males. By this time the square male too has learned much from his youthful rival and is primed perhaps too often to exploit his newfound advantage as a successful black male in short supply.

On the theory that mental health statistics are a reflection of psychological conditions, we examined outpatient figures compiled by the National Institute of Mental Health. Not only did we find that black males violate at some stages of life the tendency for females to seek outpatient mental health care in greater abundance than males. When measured against Psychoanalyst Erik Erikson's Eight Stages of Man, their mental health usage rises at interesting points. The black male's mental health outpatient figures mushroom at a different stage than is the case of the black female. The black female's problems are apparently compounded most during the young adulthood stage, when the most crucial personal challenge is to make a satisfactory love relationship, in the Eriksonian vein, to manage the dilemma of attaining social intimacy and maturity versus isolation. In other words, the black woman shows the strains of the bio-cultural feminine goal of achieving a satisfactory relationship, to be chosen by an acceptable male, to be validated in the need to feel desired and desirable.

At the point of young adulthood, the black woman finds that many of her most eligible males are locked in prison, away in the military, or elsewhere on the treadmill that depletes his numerical supply. The black male's mental health problems by contrast skyrocket as he is approaching full maturity, on the threshold of middle age, when, according to psychoanalytic theory, the human challenge is "to make a contribution to society equal to his potential." At this point, the black male has begun to suspect that his relatives and in-laws are right, that he just might not be able to get it all together, that he is not really "making it." His pain is greatest, therefore, in the male need for socioeconomic position or potency within the hierarchy of a partriarchal society.

However, this difference between the black male and the black female has its beginnings in early childhood when the black male may start to perceive his adulthood role of manly protector and provider for his family unit as less realistic than the black female's nurturant-sustenant role. The fact that his father is frequently not present as a natural model or, if present, is stymied in the chance to achieve the place expected of a man adds to the perception of the adolescent that the traditional masculine role is in part beyond their socio-economic grasp. Compound this with the fact that he is more exposed to the culture of risk taking, of gambling and bravado, of impulsivity and the masculine element of daring and adventurism that so often takes the place of masculine financial privilege in the ghetto. But this difference in the socialization of males and females is virtually universal, merely compounded for blacks. Not that the black male isn't socialized into society's goals of success; it is only that he may be inclined, in the absence of access to realistic avenues to success, to develop fantastic and unreal schemes such as hazardous business dreams, clinging too long to unrequited hopes of superstardom as a professional athlete or a jazz musician, what we might call the dream-scheme complex. This has the potential for obstructing and pre-empting his devotion to the necessary day-to-day endeavors in the mundane world, the routinized occupational sphere. It also adds to an impression of his personal inadequacy, of his instability and insincerity, reinforcing the legitimacy of the scorns and complaints, of the accusations, hurled his way by inlaws, his mate and the hammer of social opinion.

Yet all the while, the black male may be working overtime, "struggling," as he sometimes says, but getting nowhere fast, showing little in the way of achievement befitting his capacities, floating down the scale of occupational mobility, while losing and quitting a variety of coveted jobs. He see his problems as resulting from the racist system in such a way as to externalize every portion of the responsiblity for his fate away from himself. Conditioned in the masculine culture of war and war games, he is more inclined, by comparison to the black female, to be at war, in combat with the system that rejects him. "What happened, Booker?" his mate may wonder when he suddenly leaves his job. "They made me mad," is all that he may say. A man is not taught to tolerate authority figures who mistreat him, doesn't know the female's silent suffering, her capacity for emotional pain. At the same time it is he who is the primary threat to the white male oppressor, and this is a social reality that will too often elude the succussful black woman in these times of feminism. The successful black woman will prevail upon the faltering black male to face up to (accept) the economic and political reality in which he lives; and so, he may come to feel himself at war with the system and his mate, regarding them both as united somehow against him. All the rage that he is powerless to exact upon the system, he will rain on her. For she emerges, in his mind, as an appendage to the white man and his system.

Blues for Snow White: The White Woman/ Black Man Attraction

There is a danger in going against what people regard as progressive wisdom: you will be thought to oppose progress—in this case to be a "racist in reverse"—even when such critics secretly agree with you. For instance, many black women who complain about the black male's stepped up rate of marrying white females, condemning the practice out right, will suddenly catch themselves and, in a simultaneous breath, declare that a person should marry anybody he chooses, or in the next breath, that it doesn't matter to them, the black women who complain, who the black man marries.

Yet any group seeking to build upon its unity and cohesion—Catholics, Black Muslims when they were strongest, and now leading Jews, not to mention white people as a whole, will discourage out-marriage. Currently, when according to Census Bureau reports, the marriage of blacks and whites has doubled since the black consciousness of the late 1960's gave way to white feminist ideals as fad and fashion, in the mass appeal of pop culture, black males have married five times the rate at which the black female has done so. A report issued by the American Jewish Committee in 1979 revealed that intermarriage had tripled in the 1970's.

What concerns the Jewish officials is that, in the majority of instances of intermarriage, the Jewish partner is lost to the faith. This combines with the current low birth rate among Jewish couples to fan fears of a drastic decline in the Jewish population in the United States.

Recently, therefore, Rabbi Sol Roth, new president of the Orthodox Rabbinical Council of America, has recommended that Jews "eliminate from Jewish communal life all persons who marry outside the faith" (which includes you). Rabbi Roth goes further and also proposes to purge the rabbis who perform the ceremony. The rabbi further revealed that the Rabbinical Council of America would exercise its veto power against the selection of such individuals in organizations such as the Synagogue Council of America and the Conference of Presidents of Major American Jewish Organizations.

Although Rabbi Alexander M. Schindler, president of the Union of American Hebrew Congregations, stands considerably opposed to Rabbi Roth's plan, he nevertheless agreed that it is true that intermarriage is a threat to Jewish survival, and that that Reform movement is as upset about the situation as is the Orthodox and that they too will discourage intermarriage. However, Rabbi Schindler makes it clear that "one can oppose intermarriage and seek to mitigate its spread without pillorying the intermarried. " We hear you.

We also have come independently to the reluctant conclusion that intermarriage threatens our group today, as almost any aware black individual will agree. Intermarriage stirs in us deep tendencies of disunity, alienating further the black male and the black female. If you question a stone black feminist, in fact, from Michelle Wallace on down, she will employ the white woman/black man romance as one of the major issues that impelled her to anguish sufficient to make her cross over to join the white feminists herself. It is as if she determines that if I cannot have the black man like the white woman, I too will choose the white woman like the black man does; I will be chosen white like the black man who is chosen by the white woman. In other words, if I can join the white woman, if I can be white like the white woman, I too can subdue and possess the black male. It is a poignant psychology.

That is why we must put an end to the shameless and unnecessary tendency of too many brothers to be increasingly lost to the white woman. It simply isn't any longer necessary, now that black brothers know better and are aware of the beautiful and endless array of black women in today's society. The black man must declare the white woman off limits and begin actively to resist her. For, because of her own male shortage (not so severe as the black shortage of course, especially in the upper levels of the middle class), the white woman comes over to rip-off some of the choice black males (see our "Revolution without a Revolution: The Psychosociology of Sex and Race," *The Black Scholar,* April, 1978). Even when she is not a college person, figures show, the white woman prefers to marry the college level black male. By contrast, the white woman herself who intermarries is likely to be one rejected by fate or white male choice or both. But outnumbering the black male, say 13 to 1, if two per cent of the white females come over, that's more than a fourth of the black males gone, worse at the top. So it's no longer necessary and the white woman must begin to be regarded as offbounds. If you don't want to sleep in the harlot's bed, don't go near the harlot's door is a motto that will be our guide.

So from this day forward, starting Juneteenth of 1984, to give grace time, we must begin to find ways to ostracize and negatively reinforce those black brothers (and sisters, should they begin to take up where the brothers leave off). Unfortunately, for it is sad to say, we have no organized communal life that is coveted enough by African-Americans

107

who intermarry as Jewish communal life is important to Jews who intermarry, no attachment sufficient to our culture to cause us pain, though Kwanzaa, an African-American holiday celebration, and Kupenda love groups comprise a start. Indeed, the sisters say that ostracism is difficult precisely because brothers who take up the white woman willingly and voluntarily isolate themselves. But ostracism is only one form of shaming, and where there is a will there is a way.

Oh you will hear loud croccodile cries of concern for the brother—and what about the poor little white women who will not be accepted. Others who prefer the continued suffering of the many over the potential inconvenience of the relatively few who will be impelled still yet to choose to marry white, will jump harmonious and speak suddenly of "unity." But V.I. Lenin already knew that it is necessary first to divide and then unite; otherwise you can never remove the obstacles that stand in the way of unity in the first place, if your quest for unity requires you to embrace all and sundry of the starkest sources of disunity. It is not enough to assert the ideal of acceptance of divergent forces; it is also necessary simultaneously to protect the black race and its unity from the forces and factors that would divide us by design or indirection.

Then there will be those seeking undying love for the white liberals, and that is one thing, but it is necessary to resist malignant liberalism, especially that liberalism which would block our view or throw themselves between us and the enemy, for whatever reason in whatever way. It is necessary to confront and chastize arrogant liberalism in order to get to the enemy. Aided and encouraged by white liberals, we prefer to throw remote haymakers at South Africa, when a jab or two, let alone a barrage, unleashed in the land of the free might bring us to the place where we could really be in position to help South Africans and other distant places.

"Yeah, but what about the white woman?" a sister inevitably asks. "Why does *Black Male/Female Relationships* focus so hard on the white woman?" Not only do we reflect the focus exhibited by black people in private places; the white woman happens to be the one who is center stage as the white man's decoy, the fox that is stealing our black male turkeys. Why not ask the loving fox to stay out of the turkeyhouse instead of condemning us when we resist the practice of inviting foxes in for Sunday supper?

Oh brothers and sisters, who will have a heart for black people? We protect everybody but ourselves. Nordholt, the Swedish historian who in the early 1960s came over and wrote *The People That Walk In Darkness* (referring of course to us) marveled at the incredible irony that history will record in recalling how we have taken up the white man's professed ideology, such as a turn-the-other-cheek Christianity, and outstripped him in the worship of it. While we turned the other cheek, he kicked us all the while on the other two, took up the sword and launched the holy hell of the Holy Crusades to get people to turn the other cheek. Then, alas he found us, to take up the sword for him. Who will have a heart, one moment of sympathy, for black people? How can we lose these blues for Snow White?

The black woman suffers, no doubt about it. Will we care about the black woman? She is compelled to see the black man's choice of a white woman as a personal rejection of her, which too often it is, and always in effect. The black male's psychosexual hangup on the white woman, aside from the simple shame and pathos of it all, acutely pains the black woman in part because so much of it is unconscious or, as the philosophers say, phylogenetic rather than ontogenetic. In other words, the black woman as the

109

individual may be happily married but, inasmuch as racism rejects a black person on the basis of her or his physiognomy, on the way she looks, the choice of a white woman by a black man cuts the black woman in the roots of her feminine need to arouse the male.

It's a sin and a shame, besides, when some white wretch will call up in broad daylight to gloat over the airwaves, in the same week in both San Francisco and Washington, D.C., about the nature of a perceived black male fetish for the white female. It is unspeakable that a brother would have the gall, as some of them will, to conclude and even to utter, with clear impunity, that he would rather have an ugly white woman than a pretty black woman, then prove it. Oh people, where is our sense of shame? Did they take our love by taking our shame? Will the assertion of our strengths be enough without a simultaneous sensitivity to shame?

There are brothers who claim to be getting back at the white man, or checking out to prove incorrect false fantasies presented in reference to the white woman. Others subtly imply that they are living out their anguish, working through it, with their mothers through their conflicted struggles with black women and their harmonized approach to the white woman, in that their mothers have been the first in the line of black women who denied them pleasures and caused them pain. A corollary to this is that the white woman is freer with her favors, more compliant. Those of a psychological bent will even opine that they never had, or even that black men as a whole never had, positive black males as models. In the name of sanity, what will we not do except support and love our own? What excuse will we give, what rationalization will we fathom?

There will be detractors who wish to disdain to resist the peril of the white woman by complaining in the name of blackness that we are too hard on the black male, placing

110

once more the individual black male's feelings above those of black women and the race. He has made a choice to take his lumps in the arms of the white woman; we have not. Besides, the brother already suffers, guilt if not shame, especially when his white woman insists on accompanying him down front during black culture week programs, especially if he once was an advocate of a blacker-than-thou philosophy. Indeed, he will protest that he remains essentially black but it is simply that, like Jack Johnson, who loved two black women too hard and unrequited, erroneously gave up on black women as a group and went over to white women in simple compensation for this feeling of failure as a lover of black women. Then, while whites as a group reject him and give him a hard way to go, a white woman arises to soothe him, to nurse the wounds exacted by her race.

You must understand that these emotional wounds were inflicted, in the black male lover's mind, by his biological inferiority, the basis upon which he was said to be rejected as he lived and grew from infancy through all the stages of psychosexual development. Hence, nobody but a white woman can fully issue him a reprieve; nobody can accept him as effectively as the white woman because, unsure of himself and his racial grounds. He is accepted as an individual but rejected in his groupness, his ethnicity. By contrast, to be accepted by a white woman leaves him accepted in his ethnicity, that is his physiognomy, and rejected by black people (he is able to rationalize) precisely because he is accepted by the white woman.

Meanwhile the white woman appears as the good prisoner-of-war guard, or the bad guard on a happy day, in a program of fractionalized psychological terror of rejection and acceptance employed by those who practice institutional brainwashing or coercive persuasion. It amounts to the old kiss-kick principle black pimps had practiced for

111

centuries before white sociologists learned it from Chinese communists during the Korean War. In the Patty Hearst case, eminent psychiatrists and psychologists revealed that they still know less about brainwashing than the ordinary street pimp, the street pimp who exacts on the black whore a pathological form of what he instinctively senses the system does to him.

So we are aware that the white woman who comes over to soothe the black man can be nice to him, when it suits her, or seems so in his mind by the process of psychological multiplication, how before the brother knows it he is swallowed up like a piece of forbidden fruit. Thus, we will not seek to wreak total vengeance on the brother, for vengeance is the Lord's, and as Malcolm warned, any Negro is a potentially black person. But we must halt this shameless trend toward the desertion of our already neglected black womanhood for Ms. Anne. We must begin to systematically discourage intermarriage, evolving a taboo, an aura, to be passed on to the young black boys. We must find ways to shun and shame anybody who henceforth takes up with a white mate until such time in the unforeseeable future when it is no longer counterproductive, when there is no longer a need to resist white deception (whether conscious or not); until such time as black people are no longer oppressed by white people. Only then can the black person's choice of a white mate propose to be unambiguous.

Why Black Women are Turning to Suicide

Today, psychoanalytic insight has been backed up by sociological research to corroborate the observation made by Sigmund Freud, in his *Group Psychology and the Analysis of the Ego* to the effect that, when we choose a mate, we select someone to complement our ego ideal. We choose our "better half." Opposites attract, as they say in the streets. But when your better half has violated your rawest sensibilities, the feeling is like being attacked by an integral part of yourself, as if your ego has turned upon itself, arousing still yet unresolved emotions and conflicts with your first love objects, the parents, particularly the parent of the opposite sex.

There is so much more to it than that, as we shall see, but there are only two sides to the coin of violent death— homicide and suicide. Some theorists have even claimed that suicide represents an unconscious wish to homicide. But let us not be merely psychological; we are about to discover and present to you a sociological law based on the etiology of the new rise in suicide rates among black women, especially the young black women. Although we are dealing with age-old phenomena—suicide and homicide—we are on to new developments, when we take up the study of the new proliferation of suicide among a people, black people, who previously shunned this essentially non-African solution prior to the rise of world wide/ Europeanization.

So let us keep an open mind, free to learn from whatever sources we can find a portion of our understanding. We must use or employ the tools, the total armamentarium, of psychology, sociology, historical analysis, economics, and the politics of power. We cannot afford to rest our case on either one of them alone; we need them in a composite as we need the combined ingredients of a cake. Marx, for all his insight and wisdom, could have profited from individual psychology, to help explain the individual differences, why some develop the proper consciousness while others cling to "false consciousness." At the time of his studies, psychology was a very young discipline. Freud had not yet popularized the uses of the unconsciousness. So that Marx could predict that capitalism would generate so much misery as to move the proletariat to rise up. Actually, in times of misery that is too severe, people tend to grow apathetic, demoralized, immobilized, filled with intransigent despair. Apathy and escapism are their basic attachments. Thus crackpot militants who scorn the study of psychology on grounds that it is conservative are restrained by narrow vision, do not see that all disciplines within an oppressive society are essentially oppressive. This is no less true of economics than of psychology. What we must do is take the best of what is available from whatever source and leave the rest alone in the process of placing all knowledge in the service of social change.

But we digress. We are dealing here with the new upturn in the suicide of black women. But just as we cannot understand a problem brewing among black females apart from black males, we also cannot understand the emergence of suicide apart from homicide. What suicide presents to the black female, in fact, homicide presents to the black male today. You can't understand one without the other. Let us take up the matter of homicide first.

According to computations we have made of data presented in a Chicago Reporter study, circa 1975, the black woman is about nine times as likely as the white woman to kill her mate. We will understand the reason why. Permit us first to point out that our own systematic, in-depth psychological and sociological interviews conducted among black women found them feeling provoked to such violence by their males and that their own was retaliatory and primarily in self-defense. In any case, the white female was less likely to kill the white male than the white male is to kill her, while within a romantic entanglement, the black female was almost twice as likely to kill her mate as the black male was, or is to kill her. However, when motives are not restricted to love triangles, "black males (70.3 per cent of all males killed) are overwhelmingly the killers (78.5 per cent)." By contrast, 92 percent of the black persons killed by black females were not females but also black males and "black women comprised 87.3 per cent of all female offenders" in homicide cases. Homicide in Chicago and elsewhere in this country appears overwhemingly a matter of young black males in their 20's killing other young black males and, too often, leaving one or more young black females alone and broken-hearted.

But let us not get bogged down in figures and sentimentality. For we are about to discover a crucial social fact. Psychiatrist Frantz Fanon has already suggested that oppression breeds jealousy, envy, suspiciousness and mistrust as well as rage. We also know that the long-emergent but only recently celebrated black male shortage has ushered in new sorrows. But there are other reasons why the black male finds it hard to keep his commitments in his love relations to such an extent that the black female is increasingly impelled to seek resolution in the impulse to kill and, sometimes more recently, to die.

Now it is hard for most of us, including scholars and intellectuals, to get to the bottom of the deeper issues.

115

Among other things, we are restricted and restrained by the statistics white scholars make available to us. They will tend to present the data in a way to conceal those things they wish not to acknowledge or the grantmakers are inclined to pay them to minimize or skirt. When it suits them, for instance, they will use ten-year time periods to skip over shorter trends such as occurred between 1965 and 1970, when the movement for black consciousness provoked a brief period of restabilization in black marital stability. Along with the white feminist contention's replacement of the late 1960's black consciousness movement's place on the center stage of popular cultural reform came a sudden corrosion of marital stability for all American groups. This put an end to the generally overlooked restabilization of the black consciousness movement. Out of the genius of our people, the black consciousness movement had instinctively sensed that, within a patriarchal society, there can never be a psycho-socio-economically thriving black race without a psyco-socio-economically thriving black male. All this was wiped out by the sexual-feminist liberation movement. Since 1970, all racial groups experienced a sharp decline in marital stability, especially the black female.

The black female continues to show the sharpest fall in marital stability—and there is more to that than meets the eye. To the same extent and at the same time as the black woman has experienced an upturn in her occupational mobility, she has suffered the heavy price of a crumbling sexual and emotional satisfaction.

Now, white statisticians and their black imitators are fond of hiding the black male's special socio-economic, depletion. One way in which they do this is by ranking the median income in order to stress that the white female is beneath the white male in economic stature and, indeed beneath the black male as well, with the passing acknowledgement that the black female is at the bottom. This methodology ignores the culture of patriarchal expectation wherein even a white feminist prefers a man with some money or position. It also feigns ignorance of the well known sociological concept of relative deprivation. Relative deprivation teaches that if you have $4,000 in Chitterling Switch, Georgia, you may be well-to-to, but not in New York City. A female in a patriarchal society such as ours is more highly regarded by just about everybody than a male with $4,000, and they will experience a different psychology.

Those intellectuals familiar with the philosophy and the history of ideas will sometimes forget that a similar rank order approach to social analysis was employed during the early part of this century in the controversy over I.Q. and race, or race and intelligence (see illustration below). It was then popular to rank the figures and see that the White Northerners exhibited the highest scores on I.Q. tests followed by the black Northerners, then the white South-

RANK ORDER

MEDIAN INCOME	I.Q. SCORES
White males	White Northerners
Black males	Black Northerners
White females	White Southerners
Black females	Black Southerners

erners and, finally, the black Southerners. Social scientists typically concluded, therefore, that intelligence was indeed tied to heredity and race more than environment and social experience, in that no matter which region a statistician takes whites score higher than blacks. Wasn't this evidence of the primacy of race and heredity? With the emergence of the politics of liberalism subsequent to world war and mass urban migration, it become more acceptable in scholarly circles to look at the figures in a different way and conclude that inasmuch as the black Northerners excelled the white Southerners, intelligence was not a matter of race and heredity but rather of environment and opportunity!

The figures hadn't changed—only the culture or the norms of scholarship. Our computations from The Social and Economic Status of the Black Population and the United States: An Historical View, 1970-1978, reveals that when we employ the concept of relativity (inasmuch as all things are relative), we discover that the black female is unique in having changed her relative full-time median income appreciably since mid-century. But—and here is the tragedy—she is also unique in having changed her relative suicide rate: and she has changed relative income and her relative suicide rates to about the same degree.

Let us be quick to see this sociological law: Without a partriarchal society, it is suicidal to elevate the oppressed (black) female's economic attainment without also raising the oppressed (black) male's economic condition. Part of the evidence behind this social fact or law is widely known. The Department of Health, Education and Welfare's (Office of Health Research, Statistics & Technology) volume on Health, United States, 1979, reveals for instance, that "almost a third of the black females showed a level of distress comparable to that reported by three-fourths of an independent sample of mental health patients. These findings would suggest that more than half of the black female adult population of the United States lives in a condition of psychological distress rather than psychological well being. "Black women will tell you, if you listen to them, that much of all the stress they ever feel is fired in them, one way or another, by the behavior of the black male as a social type and, in particular, by their personal mates.

118

Let us understand this matter well. We must close our eyes to nothing, and must be up, and stay, on our P's and Q's, brothers and sisters. Out patient mental health figures confirm our theory in revealing that the black woman's relative out-patient psychiatric challenge, according to psychoanalytic theory, of making a satisfactory love adjustment, meeting the challenge or dilemma between the poles of social intimacy versus social isolation that confronts the human being in that passage of life. Predictably, this also is the conspicuous stage of the black woman's new suicidal explosion. At this point, she not only faces a depletion of the black male marital supply by jails and prisons, addiction, homicide, polluted occupational situations, unemployment, underemployment and the dereliction of psychological escapism; she also must contend with the decimation of the young male's ability to hold to his romantic and sexual commitments today.

We will not learn much about this by focusing upon the internal forces or intrapsychic conflicts such as the sexual romantic sociopathy that grips too many unsocialized males (or those of distorted or unfinished socialization) in the urban slums and their inability, even as they move into the middle class, to love completely. This tendency is epitomized by the pimp, but reflected to some extent by all the narcissistic individuals who adopt the Superfly or jive cat demeanor. Having given up on the early childhhood wish to feel loved in a matrifocal existence, these narcissistic males will focus instead upon the task of loving themselves and, collaterally, exacting multiple and continual proof that they are loved by women.

Within the context of the sexual liberation inherited from the white-liberal-radical-moderate-establishment-coallition, the black female has been impelled to contribute to the young black male's dilemmas in sexual-romantic commitment. The black female is driven all the more, persuaded

119

of the black male shortage as she is, to covet and pursue the black males that are eligible and, in the process she obstructs the black male's ability to give total commitment to any particular one of her sisters.

From the standpoint of history (a sense of which black intellectuals have seemed to lose, despite their preoccupation with the relatively safer, by-gone past), we can make use of an assessment of the consequences of socio-biological factors. It is popular now to deride the use of sociobiology on the face of it because it has been misused (aren't all sciences?) by the oppressor; but this is just as short-sighted, as we have already suggested, as ignoring biology which also has been misused, or psychology, sociology, or even economics itself.

Permit us, then, to return to our analysis of the evolution of the black male-female sexual-romantic dilemma. Historically, through millennia of evolutionary change, the female has throughout the animal kingdom—induced by the pain and responsibility, the fear, suffering and consequences of pregnancy (sometimes leading to death)— slowly evolved a certain ambivalence toward sexual endeavor. This ambivalence was moreover cemented by the cake of custom. With the development and popularization of the pill and the normalization and proliferation of abortion, even the denigration of the maternal role itself within the widsom of sexual-and women's liberation, the female has been abruptly released from her sexual moorings. In contrast to the long evolution of the female's reluctance and resistance, the male has had no time or preparation to develop and hone his faculties of sexual resistance. He— especially the comparatively rare and coveted upper-middle-class black male—is like a hungry child in a candy shop. He is unable to resist the multiple goodies. This is not to say that he doesn't try, but in doing so these days, he is at a disadvantage. Increasingly, he will be entrapped by the

120

monogamous but multiple love of too many women. Some insist that it is approaching a battle royal, and there are those who confess to exploiting their newfound circumstances of sexual-romantic privilege. We must help them to know the pain they bring to the young woman. We must help the black men to live so that the black woman will not die.

(Note that although the relative suicide rate for black females is increasing, the male rate remains higher in absolute terms, characteristic of industrialized societies. A quiet-kept secret is that it is the young black male in his late twenties whose suicide rate has mushroomed most shockingly since the rise of unisexualization. However, that is the subject of another work, in progress).

PART III: The Reconstruction

Who Killed Black Sexuality?
Reveille for a Lost Africa

A genuine sexual superiority of black people has been cunningly trivialized, defamed and blatantly distorted by white stereotyping; so that people will think that we are walking on the wild side, playing with philosophical fire, in daring openly to discuss this historic subject. The sexual superiority of black people is a subject nevertheless bantered about perennially behind closed doors, like so much unwanted debris secreted beneath the scientific carpet. This deceptive trivialization, as accomplished by white supremacists, long suggested that black males were, are, superstuds equipped with the most gargantuan sexual apparatus (hoping thereby to frighten Ms. Muffet); that black females were, are, oversexed (hoping thereby to justify the white male's historical rape and sexual plunder).

But never mind the white man's mythomania, a thing that has backfired on him anyway. White men by now have begun to believe their own crude conceptualization of real sexual and physiological differences between the races. Their impotence rate is rising with their feelings of sexual inferiority as their women began to make new demands upon their sexual standards. Black men also began to seize upon this rare white concession of inferiority and, in believing, felt impelled to make it so. White females, for their part, all the frightened Ms. Muffets of yesterday, secretly wondered too about this provocative proposition, firing in them quite naturally enough their deepest

125

curiosities.

Now concomitant with this cunning trivialization, there arose the paradoxical need on the part of African-Ameri cans, led by their intellectuals (on the advice and promotion of white intellectuals) to deny any notion of black sexual superiority. This denial grew out of resistance to the white man's system of stereotyping contained in his ideological rationalization of the subjugation of one human being by another, based on biological determinism. White liberals, who, though appearing sympathetic, will generally see you with a good thing and want to take even that away, collaborated in this defensive tendency to deny even our advantages in the hope of white approval. This trickbag once led us, as late as 1960 (to our own recollection) to such ludicrous lengths as denying that black people were, for whatever reasons, better ballplayers as a group than whites, or better boxers; and there were even black social scientists who would poke out their chests and proudly proclaim that the notion that blacks were better dancers than whites was a racist myth or at best a stereotype.

Within the relative sanity (oh yes) of the black consciousness movement of the 1960's, we soon learned that there is nothing on the average so pathetic as a white person trying to dance—despite your Average White Band and John Travolta. Indeed, John Travolta himself, though taught and choreographed by a black, is the epitome of the white race's ultramechanical or technical approach to all that is good, even if occasionally accomplished, as in Travolta's case, with rare finesse. We can see this phenomenon in a study or comparative analysis of something so simple as boxing styles and stances and the history and historiography of fashions in the handling and shooting of basketballs.

Say it loud: we're black and we're proud—and we know that there are psycho-socio-cultural forces behind it—but

126

the fact remains that the black male excels in athletics; the black male excels in dancing; and sex is a form of both athletics and dancing. We will need no courses in the laws of European logic, then, to draw our own conclusion about it.

Now what is done by paratruths—stereotypes, myths jokes, and so on—is to take a truth or a certain reality and exaggerate or distort it into falsehood if not the ludicrous. But they are based initially on a certain amount of observable reality, at least on the surface, or they lose and miss the essential ring of truth, have no effectiveness. The unschooled white observer will look at black people, on walking through the ghetto, see their lack of socio-economic advancement, and conclude that the black race is not capable of being advanced.

We can and must turn our sterotypes around, just as in the 1960's era of black consciousness, through the Principle of Stereotypical Reversal, we raised "black," once a fighting word, to a status surpassing the then lofty "Negro," which had come to be preferred by us to "Colored." However, we should restrict the Priniciple of Stereotypical Reversal largely to those qualities that rest on a bio-cultural imperative, and even then in relationship to the observable consequences of our oppression. *We should not proclaim our superiority in any regard without tying it somehow to the consequences of racism, just as we should always tie our failures as a people to the consequences of racism. To do otherwise in either case—to proclaim our successes or our failures without relating them somehow to the effects of racism—is to imply that racism leaves no mark, at least in that instance doesn't matter.*

In any case, blacks and whites alike sense something that is different about the races in the realm of sex, dancing, athletics and other bodily movements and expressions. And they will acknowledge this and call it "soul." But, unequipped to probe beneath the surface for the psycho-socio-cultural reasons, will determine that it is a stereotype and reject it out of hand. For stereotypes which flatter whites are more tolerable to all than are those that call attention to the eminence of blacks.

In the realm of sexuality in particular, the black female stands rejected by racism in her corporeality, in the way she looks, her facial features, and thus an instinctive feminine need to feel desired. The black woman is propelled, in the need to feel desirable, into a thousand secret hurts; and this feminine suffering, the resolve called "strong" in a black woman, has, through the long dark nights and days of the history of her people's subjugation, accrued in her, mistaken by the white man as oversexualization. For it was that the black woman possessed a naturalized body rhythm, a deeper bio-sexuality, even in her twisting and turning away from him, than the white man had ever known. As is the way of the male, he mistook his own sexual inadequacy for something imagined wanting in the woman.

The black male, blocked in the masculine need for potency, measured in the minds of too many women by his socio-economic position or potency (for instance Henry Kissinger and Aristotle Onassus can be sex objects but Eleanor Roosevelt and Bella Abzug cannot; Sammy Davis Jr., and Martin Luther King can be but not Barbara Jordan or Shirley Chisholm) will be impelled to overcompensate in the sexual arena. This impulse is manifested not merely in the relative prominence he gives to sexual interests on a daily basis but also in the importance of mastering the artistry of womanizing and the ability to influence his woman's behavior and sexuality, often to the neglect of the non-sexual aspects of this interaction with her. This tendency is of course seen often in white males and may be absent for the most part in many black males; but anytime we speak of differences between the races, we are speaking

128

generally of a matter of degree, of a difference more in quantity than in strict quality. Anyway, to return to our point: the editor's systematic study of forty black males and females for a Ph.D dissertation shows black women hesitant to praise the black male as a social type for anything other than this relative warmth and sexuality.

Let us not be dishonest, whispering one thing behind closed doors but professing its opposite in public places. Prof. E. Franklin Frazier, the first and the last black individual, as of this writing, to rise to the presidency of the American Sociological Association and, so far as we know, the only black person to win the McIver Award or any comparable in the field of sociology, reminded us as early as 1961, in one of his final writings (an article, in *the Encyclopedia of Sexual Behavior*) that: "the sexual behavior of Negroes, like the sexual behavior of all peoples all over the world, can only be understood when it is studied in relation to the social and cultural context in which attitudes and patterns of behavior in regard to sex are formed." Although it was fashionable then, in those pre-black power days to deny any cultural differences between Afro-Americans and whites, we are free now, by and by, Lord, to understand these matters better.

Frazier went on to tell how, in Ancient Africa before the European invasion, sexual values were a part of religious values and were associated with reproduction rather than hedonistic pursuits, pursuits now epitomized in comercialized pornography, which "isolates sex from its human context while exalting sex into a life of its own." With over-industrialization (Europeanization) of the world, sex has consistently been wrenched away, dissociated, from procreation and accordingly is losing its meaning. Increasingly sex not only is separated, dissociated, from procreation; there is emerging a sentiment that is antiprocreation wherein reproduction is invested with tones of negativism

129

on both an individual and a collective plane, so that child-birth, once worthy of a crown in Glory, is increasingly something to be shunned and at best accomplished by technical or surrogate intervention.

The Europeanization of sexuality reaches its logical extreme, but not yet its conclusion, in the popularization of the Masters and Johnson mechanistic, technique-dominated approach to sex, and the cloning, despite complaints of overpopulation, of so-called "test tube babies." This development has come on top of the subjugation and partial acculturation of Africans and African-Americans wherein sexual and family relationships were destructured and decimated. This process has been analyzed and charted brilliantly by a Nigerian professor from the University of Ibadan in a recent issue of the journal of *Mental Health and Society* while African-American professors search through Africa for antecedent sources of black family "strength." The African professor revealed how "Westernization" led to the disintegration of the African family and the social disorganization and psychological destruction that follow everywhere in the decline and mangling of family relationships. Where there once was family cohesion and community, there now is juvenile delinquency, crime and disobedience. Where the agrarian society had the extended family, industrialization brought the fragmentalization of the nuclear family.

Today, in the post industrial society we live in, the family is further nuclearized, so that a new and still more amorphous family form is emerging, though presently without a name. Meanwhile, the solutions white radical intellectuals, mimicked by black intellectuals, hold out as alternatives to the nuclear family, represent unconscious adaptations to post industrial society and will further disintegrate and fragment. nuclearize, family life.

In this context, we can see that the pseudo-liberation of

children and women (for instance, the child abuse movement) is not only a reflection of the breakdown of parent-child and family relationships, but also an illustration of the white intellectual's inept and unconsious though grandiose solutions to social and human decay. Now comprising a multi-million dollar bonanza for middle class social workers, "child abuse" grips all social classes (for it can be defined by law as emotional or physical); but, like almost every social malady, it decimates the most oppressed black strata more.

By now, many of those parents still with their biological children have grown up themselves fundamentally unparented. Having no model or social learning in the experience of meaningful parenting, they not only feel ill-prepared to discipline, to rear, their children, they doubt their childrearing capacities, even their own authority to discipline and direct their children. At the same time as they have lost the lamp of tradition, they have been led to disdain and mistrust their own prerogatives on which they must depend. Thus permissive childrearing has not worked for the white middle class either; and even so, we ought to know that an oppressed race above all needs discipline.

Accordingly, the social control of our children has been lost to the state, on one level, to the volatile and quixotic peer group and the dictates of popular culture and group acceptance on the other. On a higher plane, the agencies of nurturance and development (the family and school) have all but relinquished the privileges of discipline and responsibility for child guidance to the agencies of punishment and rehabilitation (the courts, the judges, the police, and professional correctors such as counselors and psychotherapists). Studies show the black child about five times as likely as the white child to be counseled. Authorities do this instead of helping the parents learn how to parent, now that what once came naturally enough is a "technique"

131

ripped apart from traditional learning and the emulation of one's own parents. Rather than assisting parents in resolving their conflicts around parenting, in learning to feel good and right about that role, the child abuse movement will snatch the child from the home, further disintegrating the families of the dispossessed. This is not to say that the rise of "the psychological society" (fast becoming, as rehabilitation is replaced by chemical intervention and drugs, "the drugged society") is visited alone upon the poor; for it is but a pivotal process in post industrial society and its spiritual corrosion.

Philippe Aries, in Western Attitudes toward Death (the attitude that grips other areas of human existence as well) told how once upon a time when a person died, the body was laid out on a slab in the home. Relatives, friends, community, came and went and mourned and feasted ceremoniously together. Then, with Westernization and the rise of technocracy, the practice grew to separate the corpse from home and family. A technician called a physician administers to him or her in a hospital setting, eventually pronouncing the individual technically or officially dead. Then another technician, called a mortician, whisks him to the mortuary lab to dress him up to look as good as life. Finally, when his loved ones have failed to deal sufficiently with their grief, another technician called a psychotherapist (a technician in human emotions and relationships) comes in to accomplish that.

This condition of overindustrialization, with its stripping of the ceremonial, of the social fiber, the organic connection of social relations, has led to the isolation and excessive individualism which historian Christopher Lasch mistakenly labeled The Culture of Narcissism in the book by that name. In reality, the individual himself today feels torn as well from within. The emptiness he sees around him he feels inside of himself. The fragmentation has mangled his own inner morale. Witness the rise of psychopathy such as psychosis, suicide and other reflections of personal insecurity, in addiction (perhaps a last ditch quest in part, through artificial means, for waning personal satisfaction). It is a logical extreme of our personal reliance upon technology to fill our every need or satisfaction, what could be more aptly called, apologies to Lasch, the *Culture of Euphoria.*

For, if a true narcissist is a person who, having suffered a feeling of failure in being loved, now focuses on loving himself, today's narcissist is an emperor who wears no clothes, no longer really expects to feel loved. Those who once longed to feel loved now are content to merely feel good. Thus sex is more and more important in our scheme of things but produces less and less of any lasting value, serves increasingly no function beyond its own sake. A young man says to a woman (or increasingly a young woman to a man) that he wishes to bring true meaning into her life; but all she cares about is whether he can "ring her bell." Women who used to pretend that sex did not feel good now will pretend that it does feel good.

Not that women are any special culprits here. Indeed, this cultural frenzy is even visited upon the children. Yet, having lost the ancient African rituals commensurate to the Bar Mitzvah, for example, of the Jews, we have no certain way to inform the black boy just when he has become a man. In the context of a thwarted socialization, many appear to never fully realize that they have embarked upon manhood; hence the persistence of a multitude of adolescent distractions extended far into maturity. Notice the preoccupation with dancing by middle aged blacks perennially devoted, it sometimes seems, to trying to learn the latest teenage dance craze. Notice our children of the dark ghetto walking around by day, down mean streets or on the bus with transistor radios pulsating, "shaking their booties down" to get-down-that's-your-mama, feel-good music all day long. This is far too much in stimulation and, understandably, by the time they reach adulthood, cocaine and artificial thrillseeking may be all they have in the search for personal satisfaction.

Within the era of Masters and Johnson, technique has taken priority over warmth and meaning, pleasure substitutes for intimacy and compassion. Where we once fell in love we now make love. Brothers and sisters have all too cheerfully followed their white models into the cold technology of vibrators and other such instrumentality of sexual satisfaction. Some of the sisters will even boast of giving up on the brothers as a group and choosing, preferring, to fall back upon the vibrator and even lesser technology. The only difference is that the brother will even tell you that he loves you, if you want him to. When he is truly serious, we say he has a love Jones, because love these days is a hurting thing. One is not so much entitled to any natural fulfillment as challenged to please your partner, with self worth pivoting essentially on how well one manages to perform, with hardly anybody rated a "10" anymore. You give me fever when you kiss me, but you fail to really light my fire.

Alas the African, the African-American in particular, will be advantaged by the very fact of his unassimilation into the machine culture, the machine mentality, the cold steel values of the Westernized (Europeanized) society. Witness the way in which the West responds to the challenges of ecological and environmental decay. The white race gives priority to the physical and chemical pollution: beautifying the mountainside, saving the whale or the bald eagle, the lake, the curtailment of the smoke and the smog, these simple signals of a more deeply imbedded fire. Black people, trapped in the central sections of the megalopoles, are more severely victimized by pollution, the relentless

134

physical ruination and the chemical overkill that produces it. But we also are more at risk to crowded conditions and their psychological sequelae, relegated to polluted occupational strata and conditions, to high crime areas and high criminal victimization. Our environmental problems by comparison are more social. Hence our solutions will be more social, and thereby more human. The white man is meanwhile more assimilated and socialized into a superindustrialized society and its machine mentality. He essentially has achieved domination over other races by the use of the machine, particularly the tools of war, but he has in his turn become more like a machine—in his dancing, his music, his lovemaking, his sex, his being. He is lacking in "soul" (some even suspect his rhythm and, of course, his sexuality).

The history of the white man is an ominous demonstration that man's ability to control (distort) the environment in the end is the thing that will trip him up. In the process of controlling the environment, distorting and affecting it, man becomes increasingly anti-environment, hence anti-nature. But inasmuch as human beings themselves also are animals, an integral part of nature, man winds up anti-human.

By now the white man knows and senses well his super-industrial crisis, his evolutionary dilemma, but stands helpless to reverse this process. Witness President Carter's famous Energy speech, correctly describing, decrying, the morbid socio-psychological decay now gripping a white-dominated humanity, then for solutions turning in the self-same breath to mere physical and chemical matters such as stepped-up exploitation of the diminishing oil supply.

The black race, the African, meanwhile has failed to grasp and harness the true implications of his uniqueness, his "soul," his socio-culturally transmitted warmth and

135

sprituality, which has appeared to caress his very physiognomy, his corporeality. Paradoxically, since unlike the Jew he is rejected in his corporeality, the black individual is prone to shun his corporeal advantage; he is just enough assimilated to white social values to disdain and underrate his own spirituality and his psychosexual superiority. He is impelled by the white man's example to equate and link the notion of superiority to the idea of supremacy; so that he goes on failing his historical mission, his axiomatic destiny, does not fully realize that our contribution as a race will be not so much in our sameness to the white race as in our differentness. And this would still be true, even if equality and sameness were synonymous, but they are not.

So let us come to an understanding: we will probably not soon outstrip the European in the making of machines, not to mention the stockpiling of the weapons of war, nor in shooting down the world's multitudious populace. But the very fact that we are not so much assimilated to the machinitis of the western world will be the thing to permit us to recapture and resurrect the lost spiritual force and the deeper human meaning which is fading fast from the universe, the world therein and its sexuality. Once we have grasped this fact sufficiently, and reclaimed our stolen mission, we will then hold the irreplaceable key to a new humanity.

What is Black Feminism?

In the battle waged in slavery time between the aboli-
tionists and the suffragettes (who felt that giving the white
women the vote was more important than freeing black women, men and children from chattel slavery) eventually
took sides outright with the slaveholding forces. They were
led by Susan B. Anthony and racist-talking Elizabeth Cady
Stanton. Today, in the dawning of the 1980's, the black
woman herself, urged on by a number of black leaders,
male and female, increasingly will choose to join the white
feminist camp in conflict with those black men and women
who continue to view white feminists as competitors for
the reform apple pie, as usurpers of the general revolutionary initiative.

While white radical feminist publications will air criticisms condemning the bourgeois white feminist clamor for
the ERA as discriminatory toward black and poor women,
black male militants of the women-minorities-and-the-
poor-we-are-all-one variety will go all out to push the passage of this spurious amendment in order to get their books
published, their candidates elected or otherwise to get
over in a society now dominated by white liberal-moderates
and their values and agendas. Thus history repeats itself
before our very eyes, both as tragedy and as farce, while we
prefer to focus upon a remote and ancient past rather than
learn from our own lives and our present comedy of errors.
For it is safer and more comforting to merely study ancient
Eyptian mythology, which may well have its place but can-

not take the place of combat with our present reality. Yet all the revolutionaries abroad, the Pan-Africanist nationalists and the marxist internationalists, between their plane trips to Lagos, Cuba and China, will have good rationalizations for this avoidance while their women and children caucus and hold bickering-sessions into the wee hours of the morning at grand conferences, while their women weep in utter confusion, left at the mercy of today's white oppressor and his/hers values and ideological whims. To win freedom in South Africa and Guyana has gained popularity over the unfinished struggles in South Chicago and Georgia just as to battle with Ku Klux Klan lunatic fringe is more popular than a forthright confrontation with our liberal-moderate rulers. The reason is that these preoccupations have the capacity for distracting us from America's white liberal deception.

The result is that black feminism, equal only to black women's disaffection and disappointment with the black male, has merely joined forces and echoed white feminism. Yet, any reflection soon reveals that black feminism and white feminism have much in common but even more in conflict—competition between the white and black women and the nature of their conflict with their men.

Nevertheless the black woman's anguish grows so acute that she increasingly prefers to hitch her star to the white feminists, feelings, suspecting, that her man's complaint against the white feminists, indeed his chant against the white man, is but an unconscious evasion, an empty and quixotic excuse for his own incompetence and reluctance to contend in the marketplace. Yet many of these black women resent the white supremacists, man and woman alike, perhaps to a greater degree than the black man does; and they know, on some deep level, that the white women's goals are somehow in discord, if not antithetical to their own.

138

For instance, the white woman wants to be equal to her man, and so does the black woman, but the black woman too often must long for a man to be equal to. The white woman wants to get out of the home, just as the black woman, by the late 1960's, could get a peep inside, wanting to get in the home at last to rest by day. And many black women, even now, if they had a good man who could support them and would; and if they thought the relationship would last, but it won't; if only they could believe in the black male, but increasingly they feel they can't: they'd trade the career, mercedes and all, for the man. In a patriarchal society, where even a feminist prefers a man with some money or position, where the male of the oppressed race suffers a broken or distorted patriarchal ideal, the white feminist, the white liberal oppressor, now comes over, just when the black man was on the rise in the late 1960's black power movement, to introduce a matriarchal theory and say you no longer need the elusive attainments of the patriarchy nevertheless preserved by the white man. Between the devil and the deep blue sea, as things now stand, the black woman feels she must begin to swim for herself or grab what may and hold on or drown.

When you ask black feminists what is black feminism, in the middle of some vigorous discourse, they suddenly fall silent and stammer, for they know no feminism other than that of the white feminism of the prime time news, the commercial magazines (for most don't even read alternative radical white feminist literature). Thus nobody has bothered to define black feminism, which seems strange and a shame, because white people surely will when it suits them if we don't and increasingly it is no longer clear to the black woman or her man exactly what the black woman wants. Increasingly they do not know what to say to each other and increasingly they will no longer talk.

The black woman has come full circle, caught up between a muddy rock and a hard place. She, the black matriarch of not so long ago, was said to be, along with the white man, the only free people in the world, something she could never quite get into, this freedom forced upon her unsolicited. Then she had to hire herself out to the white folks to help her man and family survive, now, she has to work both in an out of the home for the same reasons too often without a man to care or care for, to ease her personal and family burdens.

Her man, when he is around, is now too often of a mold called "macho," to her not mucho, as they say. If the black macho is not the oppressor of the black woman, as the black matriarch was never really the oppressor of the black man, what is this thing, by God, called black feminism?

Now it is true that the black male chauvinist imitates the white sexist (who has the social institutions and machinery to do what a chauvinist attempts on a personal plane); and the black male chauvinist often exaggerates the white sexist's worst and most blatant characteristics, just as the black feminist copies and echoes the white feminist. But can they really find salvation in these white definitions?

Of course they cannot. The black man for the most part has no job to give, no government to share, no laws to revise, no freedom to flaunt. When and if the black feminist wants what the white feminist wants, not to mention the new privilege of finding her psychological identity in the marketplace equal and similar to any man, she will generally not ask this of the black man; she will seek this from the white oppressor. The black woman asks the black man only to accept her when she gets her bold new break, not to feel threatened or turned off, and perhaps if he can make a greater struggle himself to be able to pull up and stand beside her.

At the very time, therefore, when the black woman is

140

getting a few things for herself, she will want some things for her man, her race, her family; but a feminism handed down from the white world won't permit her to utter, indeed conceive, these dualistic demands. But now the black woman's disappointment and despair for the black male's performance likewise keeps her silent on the black male's plight. But if there is a black woman's complaint against black men that takes on a quality that is different from the white woman's complaint against the white man (in that, unlike the white woman, the black woman is rejected as a woman and a' black), then there must be a thing called black feminism; and, if there is a black feminism or must be, maybe we are going to have to begin to incorporate it as an integral part of the black movement, though not so as to take the place of it. These things we warned ten years ago.

If we are going to incorporate black feminism, we must first know what black feminism is, just as if we are going to get somewhere, we have to have some notion of where we are going. So once more we ask the haunting question: what is a black feminist and what do black women want? Here is what we hear them saying, those who are disaffected with the black man and all but fed up to here and feeling possibly that somehow they have been had.

To be sure, the black woman wants to be able to get a job according to her ability, so as long as she has to work (for, quiet as it is kept, the notion that it is a privilege for a woman to work was sold to us not only after the woman's cheap labor supply was needed in the budding marketplace bureaucracy but in particular when two incomes grew necessary to make ends meet). Not that the black feminist would prefer to work, even so if, like Ms. Anne, she had a choice. She has to work, and that is all there is to that. But, even so, too many fail to realize, the demand for equal opportunity and equal pay is a thing she

141

cannot often take up with the black man very well, for it is a thing the black man longs for also and equally. She approaches the white man, therefore, side by side with the black man; but increasingly, spurred on by the white woman's example, she will see the black male as the fundamental source of her unhappiness, calling out in him a hurt and confused barrage of resentments and retaliatory blows. Then, just as the black man sits down to have his own cry, along comes Snow White to soothe him. The rate of intermarriage is now twice as great as it was before the rise of white feminism eleven years ago. For in the manner of the brainwashing characteristic of the prisoner of war camp, the black man faces an alternating but interlocking guardian, now harsh and rejecting, now warm and pleasure-giving and comforting. What he hates in the one he will love in the other.

In *Studies in A Dying Colonialism,* Frantz Fanon once made the statement, moreover, that the oppressor works through the woman, wrenching her free from her old customs and traditions, winning her over to his values of materialism etcetera, and through her controlling the man. And it is true that the black woman has consumed a desire for the good life, all the popular creature comforts, nice things, and the jewelry and sundry trinkets that historically have bespoken interest and admiration she arouses in the male. However, the average black woman, whether she is on welfare or in the corporation, by now retains few serious illusions that she will soon obtain these things from the suppressed and underemployed, even when not unemployed, black male. More and more, she will get these assorted fineries for herself, or she will do without, in the service of an otherwise good man that she can learn to trust, so long as it is clear that he is putting up a good enough fight, against the system or against the odds or both. She knows that the white man holds the resources and the access to life chances, that the best she can look for from the average black man is acceptance and emotional support at the home once she has won gains for herself in the marketplace. If that. For he will too often resent her for getting just as she resents him for not getting.

Aside from knowing that she cannot really look to the black man, at this point in our history, for material blessings, and despite her relative affinity to material possessions seen historically as the symbols of a man's appreciation for a woman, despite her access to the white man's cupboard, his office safe, as caretaker, clerical or servant, or perhaps because of it, the black woman secretly knows also that money is not enough. More and more, as we have said, she will have this for herself, better, and still she can't get satisfaction. After she reaches a certain socioeconomic level, money loses some credit or value as a criterion of wellbeing. More money merely supplies more of the same thing—more vacations, more trips of whatever variety, more trinkets of whatever value—so that emotional support arises as the elusive craving of the thing that continues to elude her. She will no longer ask for money, if she is wise, so long as she does not feel she is being hustled or taken for a ride by a loafer.

Low income black women, it is, true, still long for these little tokens of appreciation, some man to help her out, to give. But even her cry, if you ask her on a dark and quiet night, is concerned more with personal and physical mean mistreatment. Although black women of the middle class complain that masculine abuse is currently moving up the socioeconmic ladder, her complaint centers on the black male's failure to thrive in the socioeconomic realm and the resultant interpersonal conflict, the lack or low level of communication. What bothers her also is that when she has decided to get an education, to play the white man's game for survival to learn to relate to her white associates and their way of life, to put more of her heart and energy into accomplishing material things, she is reminded that she is no longer warm like the white woman. If she doesn't have these occupational achievements, she feels, she will be passed over or compared too often in preference for one who does—"the white woman will take care of me; she lets me drive her car, anytime I want to, gives me things, just what I want, doesn't care if I work or go to school or hang out with the boys and their women." But let the black woman achieve material holdings or position in excess of her man's then he becomes intimidated, especially those who don't have much going for themselves. Black women thus say they feel adrift, tossed and driven. If you have kids he fears to have to support them, even if, especially if, he's not supporting his own by some other woman. If you are childless, he focuses instead upon the notion of your independence, the possibility that you might be too free, that you may tend to wish to control him, that you seem to have lost and missed some crucial part of yourself, some motherly instincts and images, that you are indeed a rather strange character that doesn't have a human need for love, for caring and sharing.

Black women don't even complain that much about cooking and the wifely chores, and they are antithetical as a group to the white feminist goals of unisexism and unisex-ualization. Black women don't even want particularly to play football, don't see such things as that important, aren't trying to be men or more and more like men. Once and for all, on the contrary, the black woman wants the chance she never really had—to be a woman and to be treated like one—to be treated fairly and to have a chance to return the favor without arousing masculine resentments.

In contrast to the white feminist, who is turning back all of a sudden on the very things so far denied the black woman, most black feminists would be quite pleased to encounter the little courtesy, the chivalrous trivia, the simple and plain delight of a politely opened door, almost any kind of fussing over her by an eligible and desirable man. The black woman, you see, still longs for the things she has always missed, the gentle signs of acceptance and high regard, the old-fashioned concessions to her femininity and her feminine, yes, even her sexual worth. These things still have the capacity to please her and these things the black woman still wants.

If she had the choice between such chauvinism and a man's sure negativism, if she could have the door held open, never more to hit her in the face, she might not even feel so put down when she is. But not having the door opened, having the door relentlessly slammed when she gets there, not catered to as she once thought was desirable, neither then or now, but getting put down to boot, calls out in her an impossible depression, a lethal blow to her womanly self esteem and satisfaction.

Check out for example, this unsigned editorial in *The Black Dispatch* called "What Is Sexist?"

. . ."Much of the nation is currently embarking on a dubious puritanical voyage as far as the term sexism is concerned. Urged on by a small minority of militant females, some of whom exhibit a real hostility toward males, the notion is being sold to women generally that they must object to being sex objects.

. . . Of course, women have been sex objects for thousands of years; and their dress, makeup and most beautification are aimed in that direction. What, one wonders are men supposed to see them as—military heroes, tough guys, physical strength specimens?

. . . On one hand, women seek to be as sexy and attractive as possible, and want to be desired. On the other hand, some of them today are listening to abnormals (including lesbians, dykes, etc.) who tell them when men see them as sex objects this is bad.

145

. . . Most would agree that sex is not everything and that harassment, sex discrimination, etc., is wrong. But the average citizen these days, male and female, faces a legitimate quandry about the overuse of objections to sexism. One can't have it both ways. In the past, it's been considered a plus to have sex appeal, and normal. For the majority of Americans that's still a valid, normal concept."

Again the question: what do black women want? Mainly respect, just to be treated humanly, to share in simple conversation on a more or less equal plane without threat or intimidation on either side. The black woman longs for the black man and the black woman to work together for the good of the race, their children, their future, despite her slowly, nay quickly, crumbling hope, her now indignant despair. She is deeply pained that her man too often leaves her, that he, they, may be leaving her, the black woman, as a group. She has reassessed her demands, or is willing to, and is satisfied to accept what the black man can bring to her, if he will bring her love and acceptance, respect and recognition, these simple things she knows he can give. She will change her values, try harder if she must, if the black man will alter his attitude. To stand on the street corner and to harass black women passing by and signify in the name of stud play, to make obscene remarks, is childish. To try to force black women into returning or responding to these brash and unwanted overtures is criminal, even cowardly, for they tend to be made in the absence of any male companion.

The black woman can't understand how so many black men, instead of asking what their women want, can so readily assume that it is the same as what stereotype would suggest or what other women have taught them to expect. And while we are on it, black women wish black men would consult them on new family forms such as polygamy and all the new kinds of personal freedoms they devise in the name of freedom. For it is their lives too. Some brothers choose the women they will want to combine in their new experimentation or program of polygamy, only then to announce their new ideology. The black woman would appreciate some warning, personally and collectively. The black woman now stands warned, but black women wish black men could simply and always regard them as equals, at least not treat them like some little child, to solicit or at least acknowledge if not respect their opinion, especially when it comes in an area of their own clear expertise. The black woman longs to be recognized at home as well as in the workplace, not to feel whipped down by her man for being recognized at last in the marketplace, not to have him feel whipped down by her for not being yet recognized there. It is all so much unnecessary pain. Black women want to be taken care of, it is true, oh everlasting dreams, but not to be placed in narrow constraints, unbreakable restraints, not merely to be led, to have no say in the routine decisions of daily life, never to have a choice of movies, say. In other words, black women want black men to cut back on the double standard, and they wish the black man to understand that jealousy and restriction operate in both directions.

In spite of all of this, we have concluded that the black woman is hardput to come up with concrete demands beyond the black man's attitude, his low level of acceptance of her or his inability or disinclination to show it, or her feelings of failure in the black man's too frequent inability to thrive, a failure she too seldom links to his social plight or circumstances, feeling contrarily that he focuses upon his complaints as an excuse. The black woman thus inadvertently joins the white race in suppressing the black man's rage. So that, starting with his mother, the black man feels misunderstood by his women. Meanwhile, the simplistic white feminist anti-male orientation can tolerate no conscious demand for black men as a group, wishing instead to place the black man's problems on a backburner, to minimize and deny them. This is the paradox white feminism presents to an unsuspecting black feminism that is both alien and undefined. Having been promised a piece of the pie, the black woman feels the feminist suggestion that the black man, as a man and that alone, already has or should, or could, if he only would, if he were only willing and able personally. In the absence of any alternative theory (for none can find the light of day these days in the media or in books), the black woman will too often wish to have her cake and eat it at the same time, even if it means that her portion will be turned sour by the black male's acid resistance.

So we are faced, black people, with a challenge and a question revolving around whether black men and women are going to be able to band together, whether both can raise their consciousness, whether we can find means to raise it for them, so that they will cease to see themselves as enemies, instead to recognize their common foe, the one that continues to stand before us. Will we be able to change each other, ourselves, instead of merely deserting each other? There are black women who have given up, who no longer bother to try to date any more and black men who don't know what to say to a black woman, women who feel anything they say to a black man will likely be taken in a contrary spirit. So these black men and women, each in the their own way, are leaving our collective struggle and taking their chances with the enemy, giving up the personal gratification, losing hope of working out our dilemmas.

In a pushbutton society, we are understandably prone to impatience, in the face of chronic problems, and to look for some devices, buttons, with which to switch on a ready-made solution, even before we have come to understand the problem, feeling indeed that understanding the problem is no more necessary then understanding electricity or the chemical composition of gasoline is to the art of cooking. In the social realm, where change is needed, not to mention psychological or personal change, we will accordingly disdain to grapple with a problem in the process of solving it. But since none will really, actually, be packaged for us in the realm of black love (for it will foreordain a certain element of opposition to white cohesion in a racist society), and those that are packaged by and of and for this everlasting enemy of our people and the world (lest we forget), we keep trying to screw the wrong bulb into the wrong socket in a room where there is no light, then turn around and yet continue to wonder why there is none, why no real solution illumines our darkness, why nothing appears that we can clearly follow out of the morass of our intersexual abyss. We are swept up and rocked back and forth, torn from our moorings, between aimless infidelity, compensatory pleasure-seeking of all varieties, and the white woman peril increasingly joined by the white man's undying passion for the black woman.

In the absence of our own commitment to self-direction, the black woman's complaints are a tangled pathology of sexual and racial longings and she doesn't know where to turn but to the white world, while the black man turns half away, hostile, but as a rule too reluctant to fight, feeling too weak to build or to struggle in any sustained direction. The black woman increasingly, in this cold and frightening void, will turn to the white woman and the white man's magic, yet feel no less stunned when her man follows her example, then again when he does not and angrily but ineffectually pulls away.

So let us round out our inquiry and get on with our result. If there really isn't that much that the average black man in today's society is equipped to give a middle class black woman beyond emotional support, why is he reluctant to give even this much? It is as simple as it is conflicting: the white woman wants from the white man; the black woman wants for herself from the white world but she must also want for the black man, the rights and resources he needs in order to give her what she wants economically, physically and psychologically. The black woman's quest for equal rights, then, does not just focus on black women's rights but also includes the need for rights for black people, including black men. In the face of all of this, our misfortune as a people and our failure in the arena of love and love relations, would the black woman (could she) find in her heart to make a public demand for the black man? No, say the feminists, the feeling is that the black woman would be putting herself out on a wary limb that is too inclined to sway beneath the relentless swing of the chopping axe. It is going to be left to the black man to prove himself before she will make so grand and necessary a move, to show where his head is, to do something for the black woman, to find something he can give her for one clear moment to show that he belongs again and always to the black woman. For she is no longer sure at all and increasingly is impelled to the attitude of giving up on the possibilities of ever working anything out with him. If and when she hasn't already lost too much of her faith and hope, then maybe yes, she will take her chances again and, if he will show her the way, shout the black man's name and his cause to the reaches of high heaven. She wants to be his partner. She longs for one concerted push for correct and effective values, new attitudes and inspirations, some clear and present vision of where her race is going. But a lot is going to be up to the black man. Together they will shape the meaning of black feminism—or its meaning will be shaped for them by somebody else.

What is Black Masculinity?

In a recent discussion of black manhood, it readily emerged that there was some difficulty among the males in reaching a conclusion. Some of the brothers thought manhood was merely a matter of muscles and martial arts and the tools and trappings of machismo. Some felt masculinity to be best demonstrated in the capacity to captivate and minister well to a multiplicity of ladies. Still others stressed a toughness or rugged determination in the face of adversity or danger. All these are but a portion of the ingredients that have gone into a higher challenge or purpose of the male historically.

In a book, WHY MALES EXIST, a scientific writer formerly of Harvard University, Fred Hapgood, mobilized a wealth of scientific and biological evidence, culled from throughout the animal kingdom, to suggest that the female could have done very well without the male from the standpoint of evolution, including even procreation itself, but that the female allowed the male to exist to protect her while she engaged in the process of reproduction. Accordingly, we may deduce that the primal function of the male was/is protection.

With the rise of industrialization and the breakdown of subsistence economics and economies, the function of "protection" expanded to include that of "providing." But the primal role of the male human continued as warrior, first expanding to include the role of the male hunting while women attended to nurturing and gathering. The only

151

thing now is that both hunting and gathering must largely be executed in the realm of the marketplace. Neverthelesss, society continues to demand that the male do his fighting within the marketplace or withdraw from it, or actively resist it (in the case of those reformists or revolutionaries who choose to do so), fighting for a new economic distribution. Ideally, the black male will combine these two major challenges of fighting to thrive in the marketplace (providing) and fighting against the marketplace for a better black socio-economic future (protecting).

We may further build upon another finding or theory set forth by the author of *Why Males Exist.* That is that the female, throughout the animal kingdom, is attracted to the most adaptive male. The tall slim man, presumably, other things equal (in the mind of the woman unaccustomed to relating muscles and flab to intelligence in the male), more aptly reflects a versatile and dexterous capacity to adapt within today's society. The adaptive component, we suspect, also is the reason the male's ability to attract a woman may pivot more on his social position or social power and social potency than on his physical and personal charms. This grows out of the female's longing for protection and security in the reproductive process and fires in her a natural favoritism for the socioeconomically thriving male today. The attractiveness of the superfly or jive cat male among young ghetto females similarly results from his relative adaptiblility in that milieu or stage of life; but contrarily ensures that he will begin to lose ground to the straight male who passes him by on the adult occupational ladder.

Currently, the black male's lifelines to masculinity are being systematicaly severed, impelling all too many of them to overcompensate in the sexual arena. There is no ceremony, or ritual even, as in ancient Africa or the Jewish bar mitzvah, to usher the black male into a proper manhood. Nobody ever officially tells him when he has attained manhood, and there is generally too little to signify or certify it concretely. Today, the black race as a whole, having lost all effective controls over the machinery of childrearing and the education of its children tends to the preoccupation of our people with adolescent distractions such as the proclivity (at formal as well as social gatherings) for middle-aged black individuals to devote themselves invariably to trying to learn the latest teenage dance craze.

Black males, for their part, accustomed as almost half of them are to losing the father's presence in early childhood, and looking to their mothers for both maternal and paternal sustenance, too frequently reach maturity with deep and unresolved maternal conflicts. Such men are doomed to live out these unconsicous conflicts and maternal ambiguities in competitive struggle with their female partners. They are victims of a "cupboard" syndrome in which, reminiscent of their mothers, they see in all women, all love objects, as extensions of their mothers and a love-hate source of nurturance, the cupboard that holds the good things fed them and, frequently, denied them in infancy by their mothers. This is a source of much of the economic reliance of these men on their mates and their exploitation of their soulmate's resources. They cannot stop sucking their mother's breast so to speak. Of course this tendency is compounded and made necessary, lest we forget, in large part by the racist oppression of the black male's capacity to thrive in the marketplace and the consequent distortions the black male-child tends to internalize regarding the masculine role of protecting and providing for his family. There will too often loom an impulse to view the masculine role with distortion and disdain, compensatorily to develop rather unrealistic approaches to it; extreme and unrealistic ambition of musical stardom, gambling or related efforts to make it big, quick. They focus upon their extreme and sometimes unrealistic hopes to the extent of shunning or disdaining the mundane, day to day privation of an oppressive existence enroute to a viable socio-economic state.

On the other hand, despite the fact that, within a patriarchal society, the oppressed (black) male poses the primary threat to the (white) male oppressor and accordingly must be restricted, the oppressed (black) female also is scorned and made to suffer as well the slings and arrows of the black male's displaced rage. The bottom line is that the slave cannot be a slave and a full human being at the same time. Hence a female slave cannot be a woman—no matter how that may de defined—just as a male cannot be a slave and a man, if the master can help it.

Thus, by whatever name, the corrosion of black masculinity (or its objective components such as wealth and power) is multi-faceted and relentless. People keep talking about the vanishing black male, now "an endangered species," and so on, as if they know this fact. But nobody does anything much about it, because they are torn by the white race's unilateral feminist agenda and the goals and demands of unisexualization. Black women accordingly organize to the full applause of all of us to push their singular empowerment. But when black men, as happened in the Bay area last fall, dare to organize as black men and black men only, for the elevation of black men as such, neither Greeks nor alternative brotherhoods, many black women feared, condemned, and resisted their embryonic but long overdue envdeavors almost as much as the white establishment did. Even to this day, some brothers testify, they are encountering the wrath of the powers that be for their November participation. White men and white women of course can organize whenever it pleases them, and for the most part they are ignored or applauded by us. They are even supported, if not applauded (for we have seen that too) in their arrogant efforts to organize and misorganize black people who appear flattered and grateful for the presence and attention of the "good" white people.

We know that there is something we must do, and we must turn away enough to think or begin to think for ourselves; but what can we do to begin to flatter ourselves and one another, to feel flattered and to flatter in return? Once we have come upon the answer to that simple question, we will know then what we must do for black love.

Coping with Male/Female Alienation in the Coming Bad Years

By now the black woman is inclined to see her problem as one primarily resulting from some felt inadequacy of the black male. The black male recognizes that his problems derive from the white system of oppression, but often feels too powerless to cope and, blocked from the avenues of social power, may overcompensate in the sexual. He will be all the more a man, so help him, in his confrontation with his woman (women). If employed, instead of sustaining his relentless search for a new job, he may be overcome by anxiety and simply decide, as in the case of one fellow, to hide out in the closet by day in order to try to catch his woman cheating in the night. At other times, he is impelled to patch up his beseiged masculinity with some multiplicity of women, the very conglomerate of which prevents him from quite fully and forthrightly confronting and shaping a lasting relationship with either one. Paradoxically, many find they have many women but still can't be with someone they truly love. A brother may have a choice of women while, increasingly, the corporate sister may have a high-paying job and a sleek condominium, only to sail around in her new car and Calvin Kleins alone, wondering how blue can she get. So what happens when your eyes meet mine? Let's take the black man and woman one at a time. First Nathan will speak, for just this once, then Julia.

WHEN YOU'RE IN LOVE WITH A STRONG
BLACK WOMAN

These things are not necessarily autobiographical or personal, but they reflect our clinical study of the situation, personalized. It seems, sometimes, that where the patriarchal system encourages the too frequent tendency of black women to place the blame for their financial predicament on the black man, the feminst movement now urges her to even hold him excessively accountable for her emotional distress as well; and these two forces or disaffections—the economic and the personal—are often diffused, confused and confounded. But who will weep for the dreams of the black male? The black woman will castigate the black man for his financial failures, then compare him to her image of the white man while the white man pulls down tighter on the black man's purse strings and buckles him under a low and rigid ceiling of financial and professional resources. In the current and coming bad days of inflation and recession, the financially feeble black male will increasingly find that his woman is losing the last drop of faith in his capacities and even his enduring good intentions. But more about that later.

For the moment, let us take up the issue of personal relationships, understanding as we go along that these are shaped and affected by the circumstances in which we find ouselves but that it is too much to expect that the oppressor will voluntarily reverse himself and lift us up. That we alone must do or instigate. As Fanon observed, the oppressor often works through the woman, wrenching her free from old customs, old ideals, winning her over to his values of materialism, and through her controlling the man. How can the black man resist and keep up with the colored Joneses simultaneously? Many women are accordingly contradictory in secretly wishing their man to resist oppression yet fearing the white man's lash too hard, the threat of the loss of a job or the inability to meet the Scandinavian Modern Veneer monthly furniture bill or the second mortgage on the house. She will srongly urge other men to wreckless militancy, but it falls a different story when it comes around to her own fellow. In her relationship with the black male, the strong black woman may long to subdue the strong black macho male but, once having succeeded loses interest in him. Psychoanalyst Karen Horney, though a feminist of the Marcus Garvey era, reported finding a syndrome of "feminine masochism" among peasant women wherein they didn't feel loved unless they were suffering, apparently as they had seen their mothers suffering before them at the hands of their fathers and other men. Our own studies show that the black woman is proud of her strength, but she is ambivalent about it in that she feels her strength has largely been forced upon her historically and that her strength will someday be the death of her or at least her ability to get along with black men. It already presents too many problems, she feels, to her in relating to black males, and most black women will secretly tell you that they would give their right arm to have a strong black man to stand beside them. Yet the black woman has incorporated the stereotype and a certain reality of the black male's failure to thrive in an oppressive environment, a patriarchal and racist society wherein he poses, in the white man's mind the primary threat to him and his dominance. The black woman longs for a black man with strength and prominence, even the chance herself to be weak sometimes, to have a steady shoulder to lean on, but fears to let herself go, cannot indulge her luxurious fantasies that the black male will still be there and even then that he will be a steady leaning post in times of storm and trouble. She senses what Kathleen Cleaver has called a "broken patriarchy," a phenonmenon that was misnamed "the black matriarchy" by poetic sociologists of the post-Depression era, but it is a phenomenon, this topsy-turvey situation of relative powerlessness of the black male, which is real by any other name and must be dealt with by black people, cannot be wished or even rationalized away with rhetoric of the white liberal oppressor. As things now stand, the white feminists are clouding it over with the notion that it doesn't matter, that indeed men need not excel economically and psychologically, but she has nevertheless failed to restrain the reach of the white man over her. The white man's full time median income, relative to the white woman's, has not changed since the onslaught of feminism; it is the black male who has lost relative ground, despite a brief flash in the piepan in between World War II and the current white feminist years. Feminism allowed the white man to keep his act together while he further alienated and distorted and confused, black male/female relationships. This trend in turn impacts upon and pulverizes the black male's relationships with the black woman which now are compounded by the amiguities and rationalizations resulting from the ideals and rhetoric of an anti-male, even anti-maternal, white feminism. The white race has a woman problem; the black race has a woman problem and a man problem in that, unlike the white man, the black man is also oppressed. The white woman has only to raise herself to the level of her man. If the black woman moves up without a simultaneous escalation of the black male, she will compound her isolation and too often look around to find that there is no strong black man to stand beside her. But let us become reluctant to malign and to fear the strong black woman, moving out instead to meet her, to grapple front and center, to learn to live with her, to cherish her strength and her stalwart sense of duty, for she, the strong black woman, will rear our strong black race. Now, Julia.

THE SEDUCTION OF A MACHO MAN

I used the word "seduction" not merely to signal a discussion of how to deal with a so-called macho man but also to set the stage for showing how a certain kind of black man is "seduced" by the system of oppression and his own psychology into a perennial and sometimes pathetic self-defeat. In the first place, let us say at the outset that machismo is "an exaggerated awareness and assertion of masculinity," according to Webster's Dictionary; and psychological theory would suggest some personality disorder there, some compensatory, defensive machinitions at work. The macho, his apparent narcissism, is not true self-love but a feeling of failure in being loved. Having given up on the possibility of being loved by others, the macho has grown preoccupied with self-love in the quest to patchup his injured self-esteem. He may need or covet a multiplicity of women and some form of excessive, ritualistic obedience from a woman, as symbols of the female love he longs for but cannot feel. Others take up a psychic war with women out of a deep need to be nurtured, seeing every woman they meet as replicas of their mothers who intimidated them in infancy, seemed all-powerful and mysterious, and later withheld goodies and nurturance from their whim, kept their hands out of the cookie jar. Such men see women as an inexhaustible repository or cupboard of nurturance and satisfaction, but, since no woman can replenish, let alone undo, the lost nurturance and anguish or sense of nurturance and anguish at the mother's breast or cupboard, they are doomed forever to an infantile dissatisfaction and longing, repeating and fighting out all over the unresolved conflicts with their mothers. Romantic love, leaving so much to the unconscious, stimulates infantile anxiety regarding loss of objects (significant persons or loved ones and/or these persons' love).

But social psychology aside, the black woman is tired of standing in for too many black males' mothers and doubly tired of supporting two egos, her own and his, tired of raising one "boy" after another when they're not her sons. We can't stand the simple pain of his displaced rage too much longer, though we know the problem and from whence it springs.

For a certain kind of black man, everything under the sun and frequently things that shine above it, are blamed on his black woman. His failures, that is; for all the successes are singularly his. For another thing, it sometimes seems that black women, having been conditioned in the economics of the cupboard, with constant chances to compare the white woman's cupboard and her own, are far more frugal and watchful of the rainy day, while too many black men, the sisters feel, brought up as soldiers, cowboys and warriors, would rather stand out in the storm.

Yet the black woman is frequently told that, if she doesn't want to go along with all of his ideals, especially the economic, she'll be the cause of her black mate's downfall, why he can't get ahead, and anyway, he can get somebody else; just in case she's forgotten the recent statistics and all of his personal charms and untapped capacities. The strong black woman feels frequently that she is regarded as a mere workhorse with no time off for "strong" behavior on the job or in the family either.

With her feelings and herself neglected, the strong black woman may quickly fall into the alternative fantasy that an outside man will make her burdens lighter, even help to hold her battered and shaky marriage together, enable her to tolerate an unhappy situation, to put up with the constant emotional rain. Such sisters have learned how to keep a smile and a straight face while intermittently slipping into darkness, even as the brother is out tipping gingerly with some long tall Sally.

The problem with all of this is that it remains serruptitious, when what we need as an oppressed race seeking social change is psychological and social stability, strong discipline. Haki Madhubuti (Don L. Lee), for instance, has spoken on this need in a recent *Black News* interview, and there are essays in the wing and in the making by a number of leading black intellectuals seeking a reconsideration, for instance of the pre-colonial African practice of polygamy. But if current family forms have outlived their usefulness, we should change them by our own direction and initiative, not in conformity or adaptation to oppression, nor according to the spurious designs of the master/mistress. Meanwhile, these speculations cannot be used as counterfit licenses or rationalizations for the black male to fail his role and his commitment in his matings. But we may need sometimes to give the brother a break; for he needs to believe in himself and, in the process, to know that we believe in him. We must keep the brother alive and stepping, sisters, but there are times when the brother may need another helping hand. As soon as he reaches out for one, we will offer him the other, if he needs it and deserves it.

WE CAN WORK IT OUT
Before we evolve a solution to anything, we must first begin to understand the nature of the problem. Further, we will sooner or later have to confront the reality that is current for too many persons, male and female, to profess and even preach one thing while relentlessly practicing another. We are living too in a time when it is conventional, even required, that we will look at the world and our predicament through rose-colored glasses, that we will deny on grounds of the oppressor's crackpot psychological theories the existence of our difficulties, choosing from

163

among them what is positive to spotlight, that otherwise we ought neglect to see and, when we see, to hesitate to call out any unnecessary attention. There is a reason for our current receptivity to a pollyanna psychology. At a certain time in the struggle against oppression, whenever the oppressed begin to feel too weak to violently confront the oppressor head-on, especially when we have recently tried and believe we have failed, the oppressed will seek instead to focus on persuading the oppressor of their native worth. This cult of image-making used to frankly take the form of trying to "win white hearts and souls," before the Civil Rights Act of 1964, which broke down segregated restaurants and similar public accommodations amid empty warnings that riots would occur around integrated eating. Then came the black power war cry in its turn which taught us the role that force and fear, until then denied, will play in matters of social change and freedom. The case can even be made, and has been, that fear was the ingredient that first ignited the white man's soul that grew, now rationalized by the ideology of racism, into the machinery of color oppression after his initial, intimidating encounter with the darker peoples upon stepping cautiously off the ships. If I feel you are inferior to me, I will rush to give you the headstart or offer to fight you with one arm bound behind my back. But if I am not quite sure of our relative capacities, I will seek the advantage for myself. We struggle as black people to persuade the white man of an unheralded worth when what he fears above all is that we just might be superior, seeing as he does in a white man's logic and analysis that what he has let us into, whatever sport or entertainment industry (indeed, even while restricted and restrained, say, in international diplomacy), we proceed to dominate. So it appears that we have tried to convince the wrong man. What we need to do is persuade ourselves of our own true worth; but this

164

cannot be done by denial and pretense; for where we once had shame, we now have guilt and shame, knowing in our hearts that we have lied when we pretend that black people as a group do not suffer special problems in their family relations that derive unilaterally from their racial oppression. Besides, what trips up the slave is the desire to impress, to gain recognition and approval from the master. Instead, we must first accept the premise that we do have a problem.

If you are with us, let us face the problems firmly. Let us have the simple courage to learn new ways while remembering to unlearn outmoded old ones. The things we will need to know may be in the realm of the cognitive, new knowledge of our relationships, their subtle intricacies, and how oppression impacts upon them, but we will also have to learn new ways of feeling toward ourselves and others, new ways of responding one on one. Before we can change we must feel like changing; before we can change others, or in the process, we must change ourselves; for oppression distorts the reality of both the master and the slave.

We will need new knowledge of ourselves and our emotions. Let us start with a recognition of the black male's secret doubts and his need to feel that his woman believes in him if he is to break the vicious cycle of stereotype and personal performance. It is understandable that a black man and his woman, sensing that his success or performance is not up to his potential, let alone when unemployment hits, will both be anxious. At the very time when they will need to keep clear heads and stick together, they will frequently begin, in spite of themselves, to project the blame on the other. In the face of the black woman's criticism and growing doubts, the black male, far from being spurred to greater effort and tenacity, will languish in ambiguity and anxiety, projecting his anguish on to his judgmental mate, leaving his capacities to cope further crippled. He may unknowingly defeminize her, that is, chastize her for her failures in the feminine tradition, while she condemns crucial aspects of his masculinity. He may subtly compare her to his mother in the culinary arts, jab at her beauty by cajoling her excessive poundage, decry her ignorance of things philosophical, not to mention the "political," while complaining all the while of her emasculation and critique of him and his career strivings. He may focus upon a supervision of the kitchen and the children, as he competes with his mate in mutual and by now retaliatory criticism of each other, leaving no safe territorial imperatives, no space or turf in which either can retreat. While preoccupied in the correction of each other, they naturally neglect to correct themselves, unconsciously languishing latched in a cacophonous cycle of counter-criticism.

In his defense, let us admit that the black man's upbringing has placed him at a disadvantage, reared as he is and must be to compete in a marketplace that now blatantly plays him cheap, persuaded of the importance of being, as sociologists say, "instrumental" instead of "expressive." Even in the cold and empty environment of the anonymous metropolis, the black man will find more opportunities to be expressive than instrumental. In this analysis, he is understandably more likely, compared to the black woman, to pick up a distorted reality or develop a skewed, pathological response to the instrumental role he is forced to play at a handicap in a society that looks on him as a man-child but sees him as posing a special threat to the dominant white patriarchy.

In this context, many black women complain that the black man does not talk to her, feeling when she comes home weary in the evening, complaining at the end of a hard working day about the white man's pressures and false privileges, restraints and elusive opportunities in the marketplace, that he is somehow personally condemned. He would rather take a walk, or find a place on the corner, the poolroom or the pulpit, to pose and posture with the brothers, simultaneously in a better arena to impress unknowing sisters. For her part, the woman may collaborate, out of policies of pollyanna which prohibit the expression of family conflict. What they lose and miss as a couple are the many small skirmishes any contestants need before facing the Olympiad. Moreover, they fail to develop the feeling—itself an ever present inspiration and a tranquilizer of family strife—that, whatever comes up, whatever happens, somehow they know they can work it out.

The white woman lacks a long familiarity with the marketplace frustrations of the black male and comes out of a bag of associations with men who have always seemed to thrive there. "How sad" she thinks of her black mate, "he doesn't believe he can make it in the white man's system. I'll show him the way and hook him up with the right connections, with men I know who have made it. I'll regard him as a manchild in our promised land and wait for him to learn. All he needs is me."

The black woman by contrast approaches the black man with a long prior history of masculine failure, stretching from the mates she has previously known, to her own father perhaps in the majority of cases, to her grandfather and ultimately to chattel slavery. She too has seen males making it, for she was privy to the plantation kitchen, then the maid's close intimacy perhaps fanning flies around the dinner table conversation, and now typing his letters in the white collar bureaucracy, even if she may make less money than the blue collar black male; she sees the system working. Without meaning to, she will mimic the nagging, scolding mother in her dealings with the black man, however sweet and subtle that may sometimes appear "Careful, you may fall out of the tree. Don't go near the water . . . why can't you swim like Mr. Charlie?"

167

How to have full confidence in the competitive strivings of the black male economically is a challenge that no scientist or inventor has the vision to persuade her. But she will learn, for she is resourceful, that she too must employ the white woman's manchild strategy, approaching the oppressed black male as she would an infant beginning to walk (without at all meaning to degrade or denigrate him by that comparison; but she will rise above the handicaps of history. She will keep this secret knowledge to herself, even when she is angry).

When a child stands up and tries to walk, take one, two, maybe three steps forward, we do not throw up our hands in total dismay. "Oh how nice, look at him walk," we say to the toddler as he lands once more on his bottom. We refrain from killing his spirit too soon, his will to go on, neglect to inhibit or frighten his meager endeavors. It is the black male who must and will soon get up and walk, but it is the black female who must encourage and reinforce him in his early trials and tribulations.

The black man who has learned to feel so loved and fully adequate, to feel that he can cope with any conflict in a dying racialism, will understand that although it is true that deep in her bones the woman does not respect a weak man, the weakest of all men may be that man who, in his instinctive rebellion, even violent outbursts and explosions, unconsciously collaborates with the white man nevertheless in corroding black family relations, a process to keep a race in disarray and ever more subject to dehumanizing subjugation and control.

For this reason, we as a people must begin to recognize that our task is a two-fold strategy, to alter and improve our most intimate relations, and in turn our institutional life, to codify and unify, while in the process changing and preparing to change the entire social structure, knowing that there is no possibility of a free and healthy relationship in the fullest sense in an oppressive, morally decadent and amorphous society. But rather than fall victim to the old chicken or the egg see-saw, we will choose to face the oppressor on both fronts. As the air is filled with pollution, and the white man's culture sags in continual decay, while Ms. Anne, encouraged and backed up by Mr. Charlie, fanticizes, historicizes,and legalizes around her faint potentiality of being raped; from the banks of the River Niger to the shores of the Mississippi and the swamps of New Orleans, in one biorhythmic eruption, everlasting, we will unleash the brave creation of a new and viable social order for ourselves and our pround progeny.

The Second Stage:
Our Final Chance

Things have fallen so sadly that a counselor at staid and cautious (historically reactionary) Howard University, Audrey B. Chapman, was impelled to call a conference recently, on the campus, treating the bold and unashamed subject "man-sharing." This tops reports of a "Sweetheart Swindle" in the District, wherein coveted black males will take up with black white collar and professional women, extracting a lot of cash, then disappearing after a couple of weeks or so. The Howard therapist called a press conference and explained that so many women had been in counseling for depression and sequelae to the dimming prospects of finding a serious relationship with a man.

The therapist encouraged black women to begin to adopt an "a la carte" approach in their search for a man. In the a la carte approach, "women date several men for specific reasons or to fulfill whatever needs happen to predominate at the moment." This romantic utilitarianism is instant gratification at its nadir, promising splintered rewards at best. Indeed, one of the reasons black males find it hard these days to keep their commitment to any one woman is the superavailability of the rest of them.

A recent issue of *Essence* magazine has an article by a Howard University professor of psychiatry celebrating the joys of masturbation: "Masturbation: A Way to Experience Your Sexual Self." The article includes such embellishments of autosexuality (do-it-yourself) as using the saliva or

171

spit as a lubricant and the celebration of the potentially more abrasive vibrator, which, the Howard psychiatrist cautions, is safer at low speeds.

The situation is now so grave that there is a denial in the June, 1983 issue of *Ms.* magazine that feminism destroyed the family (or helped to, as part of the Nixon-Rockefeller unisexualization program), or that feminism is anti-family, though everybody or anybody objective enough to look, can easily see that the movement generally promotes the notion that a man should not be regarded as important to a woman and that motherhood is without much redeeming value and may be oppressive if not a curse. (See Barbara Enrenreich, *The Hearts of Men: American Dreams and the Flight from Commitment,* 1981, and "Feminine Notes," *Ms,* May, 1983).

Ms. Ehrenreich nevertheless admits, in quoting a study by Stanford University sociologist Lenore J. Weitzman, that:

> "Upon divorce, a woman's standard of living falls, on the average, by 73 percent the first year, while the standard of living of her ex-husband rises by 41 percent. For the man, the alternative to marriage might be loneliness and TV dinners; for women it is, all too often poverty . . . If a man remains single until he is 28 or even 38, he may be criticized by girlfriends for his 'fear of commitment,' but he will no longer be suspected of an unhealthy attachment to his mother or a latent tendency to you-know-what. If he divorces his middle-aged wife for some sweet young thing, he may be viewed, not as a traitor to the American way, but as a man who has a demonstrated capacity for 'growth.'"

Her complaint is real enough, but precisely a by-product of the pseudoliberation of the Nixon-Rockefeller program of unisexualization. This is doubly so for the black woman who, through white-run wife abuse centers and the like, is encouraged by white feminists, armed with grants, centers and resources, to identify her problems on a personal level with the black mate with "sexism" in the job market manipulated by white people. In addition, the black woman's complaint against the black male's too frequent displacement of his rage onto her, together with acting out behavior, is co-opted to legitimize the white woman's quest for more of the limited reform apple pie to place with her mate's share in the white family pot while our men are further denied and dissonant.

A study of 4,000 men and women in the United States conducted by a Penn State professor, Gerald Phillips, concluded that only a small proportion of women, if any, benefited from the feminist movement—the "better trained, better educated upper middle class women." This duplicates our own earlier findings as well as our 1969 predictions.

Professor Phillips might also have added, since black women have always had to work in order to help make ends meet, if not to go it alone, and whatever new occupational gains they received in the feminist Seventies have left them too often with an inadequate supply of equal-status males. However, as benefits the conformist scholar, Prof. Phillips went on to predict, optimistically, that computers will erase much of the current difference between male and female in "a muscle-dominated society." No more, professor, than the typewriter did in its day, unless computers will begin to give birth to human offspring, in which case Heaven may need to help us all.

By the year 2000, one hundred percent of those living below poverty level in the United States is projected to be women. This is called "the feminization of poverty" by feminist theoreticians who, as the carrier-group of the Nixon-Rockefeller program of unisexualization, helped to bring about the destruction of marriage and the family and the proliferation of single women parents now in the wings. The so-called "feminization of poverty" is a direct consequence of the so-called "choice" to be single they were holding out in the Seventies. Yet almost all of the members of Single Mothers by Choice, for instance, who were interviewed recently said they had not given up hope that they would someday be married.

The feminist element of the federal government's program of unisexualization is now revealed as at best pseudo-liberation. Barbara Ehrenreich, author of *The Hearts of Men*, goes so far as to maintain that the feminist movement was a reaction to a major copout by men in their own earlier revolt against the traditional masculine role as the family breadwinner. Ms. Ehrenreich is getting hot, but we now know that things are not quite that simple. However, she correctly observes that women "got stuck with the lower paying jobs as well as with all the old responsibilities that men are increasingly able to duck." Columnist Joan Beck continues the argument:

> "Who really did win? Women—who are now stuck with doing two jobs instead of one and are paid only 59 cents to a man's $1? Women—who in increasing numbers must take sole financial and caretaking responsibility for children? Women—who are now socially pressured into loveless premarital sex with increasing risk of herpes and abortion?"

Ehrenreich and Evans both point their fingers at the soaring divorce rate which pushes millions of women into poverty and welfare. The do-your-own-thing approach of the so-called sexual liberation movement, at bottom aimed at discouraging marriage and thus population growth, leaves men single and women single mothers. Thus happiliy married Betty Freidan has now moved on to The Second Stage, in which she seeks to liberate men and to calm the com-

174

plaints of women—now that the damage is done and, many believe, irreversible.

Now that women are having second thoughts, now that our families and our relationships are in disarray, now that the government has the population control program working, now that the baby boom generation has reached adulthood (and are going to need customers in the future and a big enough base population of working persons to support the senior baby boomers in old age), the manipulators are encouraging women who were once lured into the job market to take out time now before it's too late to have a child. True, this will ease the unemployment problem (other things equal), but above all, the women choosing to stop work and have children (those who have that privilege) will be disproportionately white and middle class, thereby implementing in part the second stage of the Nixon-Rockefeller population control program of unisexualization, offsetting the waning relative white population of America and the world. White feminists who openly condemned motherhood and family roles, echoing the Nixon-Rockefeller Commission, will now begin to see it as a strategy to pretend they have not been destroyers of the family nor hostile to homemaking or homemakers. But we know that they have been.

The U.S. News & World Report predicts that in the year 2033 "relationships will be a confusing tangle as a result of people living longer and changing mates to suit the seasons of their lives. The editors go on to predict that the growing trend of serial marriages will be a "normal and planned-for part of adulthood" and that the government will become more involved than ever before . . . and will also oversee the use of genetic-engineering techniques that hold the potential for altering the charateristics of babies." Do you believe they will blacken characteristics?

Further, *the U.S. News & World Report* forecasts:

"It may even fall to Uncle Sam to help increase falling birth rates, some futurists foresee the day when the government will not only offer financial rewards for newborns but also encourage more births through greater use of test-tube baby techniques and surrogate mothers."

Although this sounds like science fiction, it's really not unusual for one institution, such as the family, to give up some of its functions to another, such as the government, explains a Temple University demographer, Joseph McFalls. Little by little, they're letting the cat out of the bag, but cat and bag nevertheless continue to escape the black intellegentsia.

Meanwhile, feminists (including a lesbian center, for instance, in Oakland, California) are storing up their own sperm banks, blood bank style. Although friendly heterosexual male sperms are accepted, the lesbians are poised to secede from heterosexuals and to use gay sperms only. Thus, before we know it, they will have the sperms and gone, as it were. Indeed, Rabbi Abrama Feinberg, in his book, *Sex and the Pulpit,* solemnly ponders in an entire chapter whether the penis is expendable.

A lesbian woman, who helped impregnate her former "wife" through a do-it-yourself artificial insemination process involving a turkey baster, has recently taken her lover to court over visitation rights befitting any father. She points out her dutiful payments of regular child support since the breakup of her "marriage." Last Spring, two San Francisco sociologists claimed that their two-year study indicates that the practice of incest is not harmful psychologically and may be benifical to your health. In a paper, "The Final Taboo," delivered to a sociology convention in Los Angeles, the incest sociologist was defended by the new York *Times* columnist Anthony Lewis, Washington Post columnist Mary Mcgregory, Bryant Gumbel of the Today

Show and Carl T. Rowan, syndicated columnist, as well as Tom Brokaw. Even Walter Mondale, on "This Week with David Brinkley" and Senator Robert Dole, R-Kansas, on "Meet the Press," saw fit to hedge on the issue. When Ronald Reagan, shooting from the hip, spoke out against it, he received so much flack that White House Chief of Staff James Baker, in a rare press conferece, said that the President "obviously misspoke" and that he meant that it is "not the pragmatic thing to do."

Medical experts also are reversing their previous position to say now that pregnancy after 35 may not carry as high a risk of birth defects as they previously claimed. Additionally, thousands of men and women are now encouraged to seek reversals (major surgery that takes up to three hours on the operating table) for past vasectomies and tubal ligations. The corrective surgery costs from $4,000 to $8,000 and is not covered by health insurance, leaving out most of you-know-who. By contrast, abortion, even where there is no health risk or disease of childbirth, is covered by Medicare. Medicare recipients, of course, will not be able to afford to reverse tubal ligations of the unisexual movement's diabolical racist means of decreasing the non-white poor births while endeavoring to increase the births among affluent and infertile whites. South Africa openly and officially presents these two contrasting policies of suppressing black births while encouraging white births. But the United States and the World Bank, led by liberals and liberal-moderates, accomplish the same thing in more deceptive and subtle ways.

In addition to test tube babies and $20,000 surrogate mothers, they've come up with something called "adoptive pregnancy." The way the technique works is to transfer the ovum—the mature female egg cell—from a woman donor to the so-called mother. The egg is fertilized in one woman and transferred or implanted in the womb of another. Let us call it the surrogate womb. By any name, rent-a-womb babies or whatever, it is going to great lengths in a world supposedly wavering under "overpopulation." (Actually, more than two-thirds of the world's population occupies less than one-tenth of the one-third of the earth that is not water). Nevertheless, the technique of adoptive pregnancy is fast becoming routine in cattle breeding. Among the many scientists pushing the technique of adoptive pregnancy for humans is Dr. Luigi Mastroianni, Jr., chairman of obstetrics and gynecology, at the University of Pennsylvania, who adds that many women would nevertheless insist on becoming pregnant with their own egg cells or/and their husband's sperm—that is, to have their own baby without actually having it, or carrying and giving birth to the baby.

Today, one-fifth of all babies are delivered by Cesarian section, a very dangerous surgical procedure once restricted to emergency situations but has increased three-fold in the past 15 years since the Nixon-Rockefeller Commission launched their program of population control. Surgery is now the major form of birth control. Yet, at a black nationalist meeting in Los Angeles last February, a black man in the back of the audience demanded confirmation for the notion that African males are the most brutal in the world, considering the cliterectomies. It was pointed out to him that nobody cuts as well as the white male, especially when he is a surgeon, and that it is a matter of value judgment— i.e., whose cutting you prefer. A London *Observer* report reveals how Christianity continues to clash with African custom, for instance, around their own concept of "surrogate motherhood" wherein woman-to-woman marriages have been practiced for generations. Kissi tribesmen defend the custom not only for inheritance purposes [when a man's wife is infertile] but also because tribal law makes no provision for adoption of children."

178

Attorney Don Bwokara, a Kissi Lawyer, believes that their practice is a "more civilized kind of adoption than the Western type of adoption by buying children." Christianity, once again, is now being used in Africa as a means of cultural disruption and mind control for population and sexual control and Europeanization.

In the United States, while there has been hardly any concern paid by black intellectuals to the emergence of population control and genetic engineering, white clergymen have spoken out, for their own reasons, about the hazards for the future of the human race. Alleging that the genetics debate cannot be suppressed any longer, columnist Richard Reeves, in the Kansas City *Times* of July 4, 1983, reports that the president of the National Council of Churches was among those who are asking scientists not to conduct experiments leading to possible alteration of human heredity. Remember how the U.S. Public Health Service deliberately let black men with syphilis go untreated in the Tuskegee, Alabama experiment from 1932 to 1972, when an Associated Press reporter broke the hidden forty-year story?

Also, Professor J. Robert Nelson, of Boston University, is quoted in the June 20, 1983 issue of *Newsweek* on the new possibilities of modifying human life. "We are in danger of treating human beings as animal stock," the professor complained. Concern over unsatisfactory administrative response to their complaints prompted clergymen last summer to pressure Congress to "stop human engineering." According to Richard N. Ostling and Michael P. Harris, writing in Newsweek:

> "The clergy's main concern is the ethical justification for making changes in the germline, or sex cells, which regulates the transmission of inheritable traits. Scientists are now working to change the genes in these cells that create such

179

inherited maladies as Tay-Sachs disease and sickle-cell anemia. The healthy traits would be passed on indefinitely to succeeding generations."

However ideal that goal might seem, signers of the petition to Congress fear that the engineering changes would later cause unforeseen problems. One example:

"eradication of sickle-cell anemia genes might make an individual more susceptable to malaria. Other clergymen are deeply concerned that scientists, despite their disclaimers, will eventually seek to make more changes—in short, to usurp the creative function of God [or nature] by building a kind of superman.

Signers of the declaration included leaders of the Lutheran Churches in America, the Episcopalian Church, the United Church of Christ, the United Methodist Church, and the Southern Baptist Convention, twenty-three Catholic Bishops, two Jewish leaders, and the head of the National Council of Churches. Indeed, they were joined by seven scientists, including Nobel Laureates concerned that when it comes to altering human genes, "who is going to set those specifications?" You know as well as we do who will *not* decide them.

You must also understand that the final push in the biotechnological industry grew programmatically out of the recommendation for research financing issued by the Nixon-Rockefeller Commission, although various individuals had randomly and informally been so engaged for years, just as astronomers interested in the moon preceded the U.S. government's programmatic decision in the early 1960's to get to the moon inside of ten years. However, the resistance of the biotechnologists to a call by religious leaders to erect ethical review commissions to monitor research into human genetic engineering is summed up by David Padwa, chairman and chief executive officer of

Agrigenetics (Boulder, Colorado). Padwa defends the scientists' stand eugenically: "In a world of crime, drugs, war and hunger, I find it a bit hard to take the self-appointed censors of developmental biology." Those readers familiar with the rantings of eugenicists from 19th century malthusianism down to today, will recognize Padwa's almost verbatim malthusianism.

Among those seeing population control as second only to the problem or possibility of nuclear war (see our "Introduction" for others) is Dr. Carl Djerassi, the chemistry professor who developed the birth control pill and teaches in Standford University's feminist studies program. In his new book, *The Politics of Contraception: Birth Control in the Year 2001*, Dr. Djerassi, who owns a 1,000 acre cattle ranch in the Santa Cruz Mountains and is president of Zoecon Corporation, which is developing hormonal approaches to insect control, promotes "the paramount importance" of population control: "Except for prevention of a nuclear holocaust, achieving effective human fertility control during the balance of the century will be the overriding social action, affecting the quality of life on this planet for decades."

Writing last summer in his nationally syndicated column, and echoing Dr. Djerassi and the federal officials supporting the Nixon-Rockefeller Commission, James Kilpatrick sees two great dangers—one talked about, nuclear war; the other rarely making headlines, the "continuing explosion of population in the *less developed nations."* Kilpatrick goes on to reveal the racism behind this official government policy and white liberal hype, quoting the Population Reference Bureau report which held that:

> "The less developed countries, which account for 75 percent of the world's population, are growing at just over 2 percent annually compared to 0.6 percent for the more developed countries.

These uneven rates mean that the less developed countries will constitute 79 percent of the world by the year 2000 and 83 percent by 2020."

Although Kilpatrick threw up the usual smokescreen about starvation and the overall Malthusian line (while never voicing the need for a better distribution of the abundant resources, food and wealth or a cessation to the plunder, of the earth for profit and power), he concludes that: "My only thought is that our [white] children and grandchildren will constitute an ever-shrinking minority in the years ahead. For their sake, if for no other, we ought to study the population projections and think about the future now."

The news to Kilpatrick is that they have already been not only studying, but manipulating, these trends, at least since 1969, as a major program of the United States government and the World Bank. It works all the better, of course, if they can keep most people from realizing what they are doing, even feeling that the program (as they pick up its tenets in the winds of public opinion and conventional wisdom) is a matter of "choice" or, at worst, conforming to irrevocably changing fashion, or a program for "liberation."

Meanwhile, geneticists are crawling out of the woodwork in droves. A New York *Times* report was reprinted all around the country claiming that the number of babies born with some physical or "mental" defect has doubled over the past 25 years. The geneticists are predicting "serious" and "disturbing" social and economic effects, when in fact many of these birth defects are a product of the socio-economic discrepancies in access to diet, medical care, maternal and child care, and the quality of life and environment. Such scientists as Dr. Peter Budetti, Director of the University of California, San Francisco's Health Policy Program, and Dr. Mary Grace Kovar, an analyst at the

National Center for Health Statistics, see social problems accruing from the existence of these "mentally handicapped" individuals. "We are seeing real increases in children with some form of handicap and this is resulting in a substantial burden to society, a burden that will increase with time." Cabinet members Butts and Watt were forced to resign for saying much less than this. The National Health Survey, which determined this new social peril, is a program mandated by Congress. Dr. Budetti's program at the University of California is financed by the United States Public Health Service, the same one that carried on the syphillis experiment on black men in Tuskegee until discovered and exposed in 1972.

Reports presented to the meeting last spring in Detroit of the American Advancement of Science extolled the prospects of an emerging ability on the part of growers and breeders to choose the sex composition of animals and humans with complete certainty within the next five or ten years. Reproductive physiologist Ronald Ericsson already claims to be able to

> "dramatically improve the chances of having a boy over a girl by separating sperm according to their ability to swim through a thick albium gel. Sperm carrying X chromosomes are favorable to the production of boys. The company now has 10 clinics nationwide and seven others overseas that perform the services, and tells its clients that it increases the chances of having a boy from the normal rate of about 50 percent to between 75 and 80 percent.

This is part of the bio-medical research stressed by the 1969 Nixon-Rockefeller Population Growth and the American Future calling for federal funding of $1 billion a year and known to have allocated hundreds of millions subsequently, although most of their recommendations have been accomplished through propaganda and thought

183

control or psychological warfare.

Meanwhile, scientists at the Univerisity of Pennsylvania's Wistar Institute are reported to have produced a genetic "copy" of a mouse—on their way to the possible cloning of human beings. Heretofore, the research has been restricted to frogs and lower animals, but this is the closest they've come—one step away—from the cloning of a mammal. Biologist Davor Solter said "we did in fact produce a mouse by nuclear transplantation, but that is all I can say now." (Nuclear transplantation is where a living cell's nucleus is placed in another cell that has had its nucleus removed). Doctors Solter and James McGrath, of the Wistart Institute revealed that their team had already produced nearly one hundred different mice so far using the nucleus-transfer procedure.

In the same way that nuclear stockpiling presents both the hazard of leakage and accidental or precipitous detonation (in that what is available for use risks being used, as in the correlation of handguns and suicide rates), the development of genetics engineering and biomedical research as orchestrated by the Nixon-Rockefeller Commission risks the perils of misuse, abuse, catastrophic accident and miscalculations. Remember such scientific mishaps in the past as babies born deformed as a result of ill-conceived pills, and the development of rare forms of vaginal cancer in women following exposure to certain medical drugs?

Yet the program of population control, particularly the cunning unisexual means to it now in vogue, is a program in which liberals, moderates, and often conservatives, democrats and republicans, black and white, can seemingly collaborate.

Indeed, a number of leading black nationalists, each in their own way, are now seen adopting and assimilating to this new program of white feminism and unisexualization. Some are already openly in advocacy while others are subtle and opportunistic. They will obtain, for instance family planning grants, appealing like their white liberal mentors to the need for fairness in regard to black women or some other saintly surface issue such as halting high illegitimacy rates among black teenagers. They do not bother that illegitimacy has mushroomed since the proliferation of birth control technology in large part because such mechnisms took away personal responsibility for the prevention of pregnancy and the management of sexual fidelity and integrity.

The black nationalist establishment will belatedly find many ways, if we don't watch them, to collaborate with the white man's program of unisexualization at the same time as they continue to harp about white cultural imperialism and the colonization of black people's minds now and, especially in the early days of African colonization. Yet here presented in our own time, indeed when boldly confronted with an opportunity to resist assimilation and cultural imperialism, they are beginning to find it easier, after fifteen years of disdain, to assimilate to the program of unisexualization and population control—in other words, genocide.

One group, a marxist-nationalist group that once almost dissolved over a feminist-lesbian factionalism, has wavered to the advocacy of the agenda of unisexualism, despite their courage in taking up currently Queen Mother Moore's two major programs: 1) the call for reparations ($4.1 trillion) owed African-Americans already by the U.S. government, corporations and other descendants, heirs of white slavemasters and slavery; and 2) the demand that the U.S. goverment ratify the recommendations of the decades old Genocide Convention (the United Nations Convention on the Prevention and Punishment of Genocide), which would open the way for black people to bring the U.S. government, as Malcolm X also wished, before World Courts and other international institutions for its crimes against black people. However, the U.S. genocidal plan now incorporates a cunning and subtle (rather than merely open killing) plan of population depletion by slipping in the backdoor of family destruction and unisexualization, keeping blacks from being born at their natural pace, while gaining control over reproduction through genetics, engineering, biomedical research, test tube babies and the like, designed to favor the multiplication of middle class whites.

Yet Queen Mother's program is the farthest thing from the minds of most nationalist leaders today currently making their peace with apathy and cultural confusion while fixating on the ego-gratification of an ancient African past that has gone forever. They will continue to sit at Queen mother's feet in conference halls but keep their eyes and noses trained on their white mentors, slowly moving to ape and parrot key aspects of the Nixon-Rockefeller program of unisexualization.

Thus, despite all the huffing and puffing, black nationalists as a group are being revealed as essentially assimilationists beneath the skin. Their nationalism is only skin deep. Black marxists, for their part, have long been revealed by Harold Cruse, in *The Crisis of the Negro Intellectual*, to reflect an essential rationalization of a wish to integrate. Hence, we are left without a current corps or carrier group to resist the cultural whims and machinations of the continuing Europeanization of the world and the collateral destruction of the moral and spiritual fiber, indeed as now emerging, the very biology of the human species itself.

Very few black intellectuals, including sociologists and demographers, have heard of the Commission on Population Growth and the American Future, although it has shaped our thinking since 1969, even to the point of persuading many that "there is no turning back now," that nothing can be done to resist the programmed unisexualiza-

186

tion of the human race and the genocidal manipulation of the racial characteristics of those who will survive.

If even black nationalists fail to hold their ground against this super-onslaught of cultural imperialism and psychological warfare, if black intellectuals of every stripe so readily deflect from a stalwart course of resistance to the genocidal and destructive program of unisexualization and population control, we will continue on the road to our gravest and, perhaps, last ideological error as a people. Brothers, and sister, we are living now in a very special age, an era of accumulated knowledge amid diminished wisdom, playing in the last dazzling inning of the clash of races and cultures. We are the inheritors of a special right to revamp the course of history and ensure the survival of a noble race, if not the human species itself.

Notes and References

See Arlene S. Skolnick and Jerome H. Skolnick, "Rethinking the Family," *Family in Transition.* Boston: Little, Brown and Company, 1971.

William H. Chafe, *Women and Equality: Changing Patterns in American Culture.* New York: Oxford University Press, 1977, p. 119. See also pp. 26-122.

Herbert Marcuse, *Eros and Civilization: A Philosophical Inquiry into Freud.* Boston: Beacon Press, 1966. See also F. George Kay, *The Family in Transition: Its Past, Present and Future Patterns.* Newton Abbot (Great Britain): Davis & Charles Publishers, 1972.

Dainne K. Lewis, "A Response to Inequality: Black Women, Racism, and Sexism," *Signs: Journal of Women in Culture and Society* (Winter 1977), Vol. 3, p. 351, Table 2. Note that the citing of a source, here and elsewhere, does not necessarily suggest agreement with our thesis, as it has often been necessary for us to complete or refine an author's analysis.

Nathan Hare, "Black Male-Female Relations," Unpublished Ph.D. Dissertation, The California School of Professional Psychology, Berkeley, 1975, Table 1, p. 29. See also my "What Happened to the Black Movement," *Black World* (January 1976), vol. 25, pp. 20-32.

Nathan Hare, "Black Male-Female Relations," op. cit., p. 127.

Achola O, Pala, "Definitions of Women and Development: An African Perspective," *SIGNS: Journal of Women in Culture and Society* (Autumn 1977), vol. 3, pp. 9-13. Frantz Fanon, *A Dying Colonialism.* Tr. by H. Chevalier. New York: Grove Press, 1967.

See "White Supremacy within the Women's Movement," in History of Women's Struggles in the U.S.: An Overview." *Women's Liberation and Imperialism.* San Francisco: Prairie Fire Organizing Committee (November 1977), p. 25. See also Chafe, op. cit., p. 58.

Vicki McNickle Rose, "Rape as a Social Problem: A Byproduct of the Feminist Movement," *Social Problems* (October 1977), 25, pp. 75-89.

Beth Day, *Sexual Life Between Blacks and Whites: The Roots of Racism,* New York: World Publishing, 1972.

Wray Herbert and Pam Moore, "Ringing Up the Carter Budget," *APA Monitor* (March 1978), vol. 9, pp. 1,4,5.

Nathan Hare, "Will the Real Black Man Please Stand Up?," *The Black Scholar* (June 1971), vol. 2, pp. 32-35.

Nathan and Julia Hare, "Black Women 1970," *Transaction* (November-December 1970), vol. 8, pp. 65-68.

Nathan Hare, "What Black Intellectuals Misunderstand about the Black Family," *Black World* (March 1976), vol. 25, pp. 4-14.

Nathan Hare, "Self-Other Conflicts and Love Relations," in "Black Male-Female Relations," op. cit., chapter 3, pp. 54-75.

Jean Paul Sartre, Preface to *The Wretched of the Earth.,* by

Frantz Fanon. Tr. by C. Farrington. New York: Grove Press, 1963. Fanon himself devoted four books to the "distortion of human relations which colonialism engendered."

Billingsley, A. *Black Families in White America.* Englewood Cliffs, N.J.: Prentice-Hall, 1968.

Billingsley, A. Black Families and White Social Science. In Ladner, J., (Ed), *The Death of White Sociology.* New York: Random House, 1973.

Blood, O., Jr. & Wolfe, D.M. Differences in Blue-collar Marriages in a Northern Metropolis. In Staples, R. (Ed.). *The Black Family.* Belmont, California, 1971.

Fanon, F. *The Wretched of the Earth.* Tr. by Farrington, C. New York: Grove Press, 1963.

Fanon, F. *A Dying Colonialism.* Tr. by Chevalier, H. New York: Grove Press, 1967.

Fanon, F. *Black Skin, White Masks.* Tr. by Markmann, C. L. New York: Grove Press, 1967.

Frazier, E.F. *The Negro Family in the United States.* Chicago: University of Chicago Press, 1939.

Frazier, E.F. *Black Bourgoisie.* Glencoe, Illinois: Free Press, 1957.

Frazier, E.F. Sexual Life of the African and American Negro. In Staples, R. (Ed.). *The Black Family.* Belmont, California: Wadsworth Publishing Company, 1971.

Grier W.H. & Cobbs, P.M. *Black Rage.* New York: Bantam Books, 1969.

Hare, N. The frustrated masculinity of the negro male. *Negro Degest.* (August, 1964), pp. 5-9.

Hare, N. Recent trends in the occupational mobility of negroes, 1930-1960: an intracohort analysis. *Social Forces,* 1965, 44, 166-172.

Hare, N. & Hare, J. Black Women: 1970. *Transaction,* 1970, 8, 65-68.

Hill, R.B. *The Strength of Black Families.* New York: Emerson Hall Publishers, 1971.

Howard, J. Toward a Social Psychology of Colonialism. In Jones, R. (Ed.). *Black Psychology.* New York: Harper & Row, 1972.

Kernberg, O. *Borderline Conditions and Pathlogical Narcissism.* New York: Jason Aronson Publishers, 1975.

Hare, N. Marriage and Fertility in Black Female Teachers. *The Black Scholar,* 1970, 1, 22-28.

See also various issues of *Family Planning Perspectives, circa* 1972-1976.

NATHAN HARE, a clinical psychologist in private practice in San Francisco, holds two Ph.D's (in psychology and sociology). Editor of Black Male/Female Relationships, he was founding publisher of The Black Scholar and the first coordinator of a black studies program in the United States. He coined the term "ethnic studies." He also is author of The Black Anglo Saxons and many articles.

Dr. Hare was co-winner of the 1983 National Award for distinguished scholarly contributions to black studies from the National Council for

NATHAN HARE

Black Studies. A recent survey of black sociologists in America voted him among the 15 leading black sociologists of all time.

JULIA HARE holds the M.M.ED. from Chicago's Roosevelt University. As a teacher in Washington, D.C., she won the Outstanding Educator Award from the World Book Encyclopedia and the Junior Chamber of Commerce. While at the Golden Gate Broadcasters' KSFO Radio in San Francisco, she won the national Abraham Lincoln Award in broadcasting. Then came three years as a talk show host at KGO, the local ABC affiliate. She has taught piano and organ on the university level, and has done commercial acting.

At seventeen, Julia met Nathan at Oklahoma's Langston Univerisity where their courtship preceded their marriage.

JULIA HARE

192